FOR MY FATHER

BRENDAN JAMES NOLAN

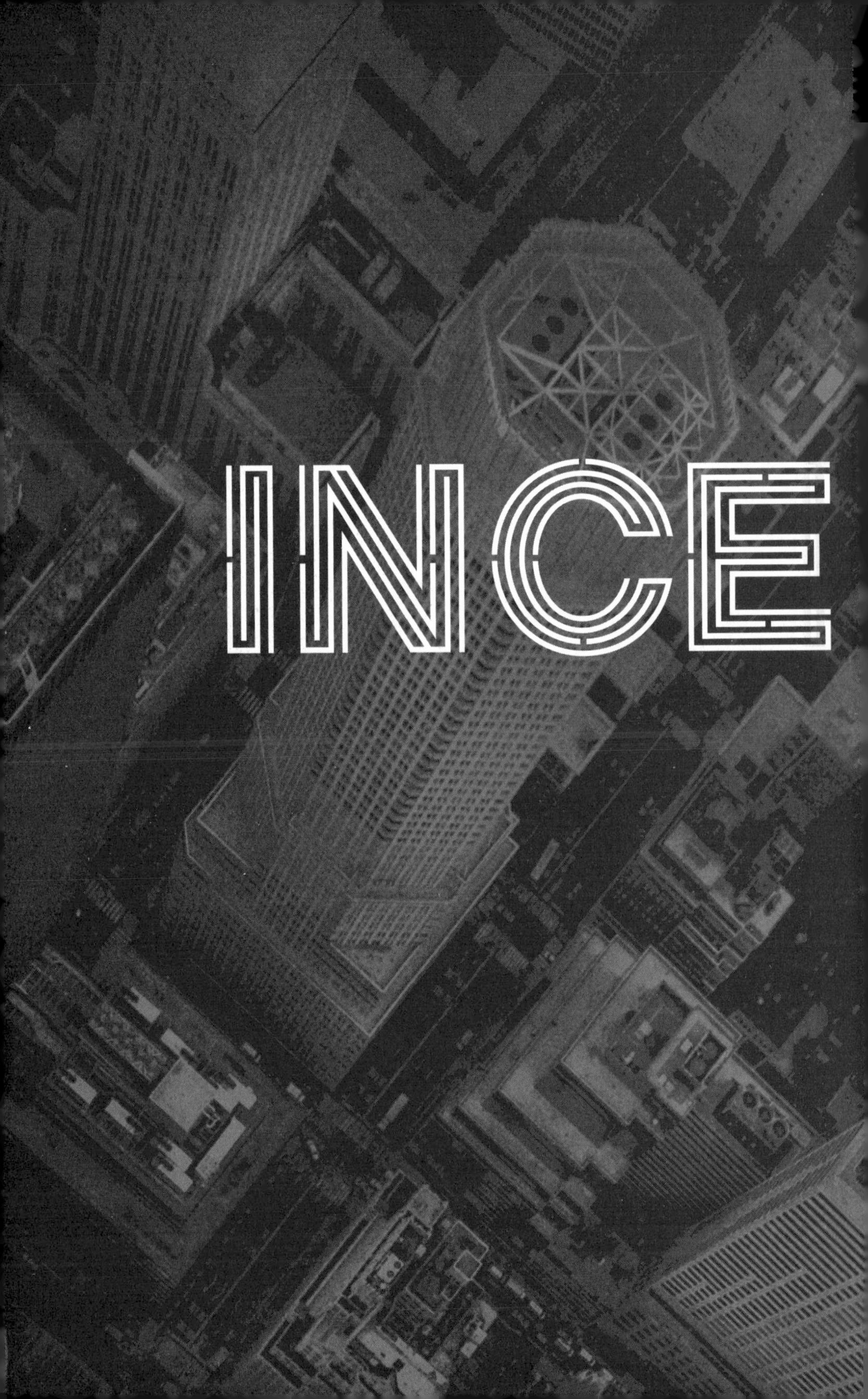
INCE

PTION

THE SHOOTING SCRIPT
WRITTEN AND DIRECTED BY
CHRISTOPHER NOLAN

INSIGHT EDITIONS

3160 Kerner Blvd., Suite 108
San Rafael, CA 94901

www.insighteditions.com

Library of Congress Cataloging-in-Publication Data available.

ISBN: 978-1-60887-015-8

ROOTS of PEACE REPLANTED PAPER

Insight Editions, in association with Roots of Peace, will plant two trees for each tree used in the
manufacturing of this book. Roots of Peace is an internationally renowned humanitarian organization
dedicated to eradicating land mines worldwide and converting war-torn lands into productive farms
and wildlife habitats. Together, we will plant two million fruit and nut trees in Afghanistan and provide
farmers there with the skills and support necessary for sustainable land use.

Designed by Michel Vrána

Manufactured in Canada

10 9 8 7 6 5 4 3

CONTENTS

PREFACE   7
Dreaming/Creating/Perceiving/Filmmaking
by Christopher Nolan and Jonathan Nolan

Inception: The Shooting Script   21

APPENDICES
PASIV Device Instruction Manual   220
Film Credits   229

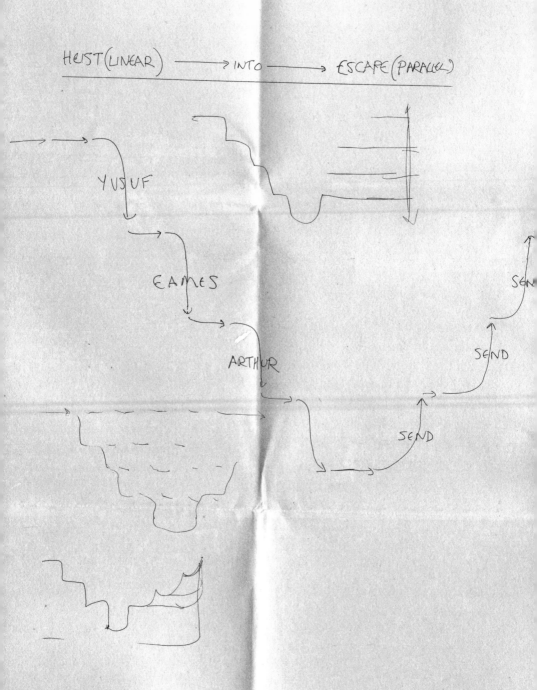

HEIST (LINEAR) ⟶ INTO ⟶ ESCAPE (PARALLEL)

YUSUF

EAMES

ARTHUR

SEND

SEND

SEN

Christopher Nolan's plot schematic charting
how Cobb and his team pull off inception.

PREFACE

DREAMING /
CREATING /
PERCEIVING /
FILMMAKING

AN INTERVIEW WITH WRITER-DIRECTOR
CHRISTOPHER NOLAN
INTERVIEWED BY JONATHAN NOLAN

Jonathan Nolan: Let's talk about the script. You've been working on this one for a while.

Christopher Nolan: Ten years, I think.

JN: Is it ten? I was trying to remember the first time you talked to me about the idea because there were several different versions of corporate espionage scripts that you were playing around with.

CN: I was. Then I took the idea of corporate espionage and applied it to the thing I'd been working on even longer, which was dreams.

I remember the initial genesis quite clearly. My interest in dreams comes from this notion of realizing that when you dream you create the world that you are perceiving, and I thought that feedback loop was pretty amazing. I remember when I was in college you had free breakfast that finished at nine o'clock...

JN: [*laughs*] That would be an important part of your life.

CN: It was very important. So you had to wake up to get the free breakfast and then you would go back to bed because you hadn't gone to sleep until four in the morning. But I would make sure I got it and then I would go back to sleep for another two or three hours. And in that slightly weird, discombobulated sleep I discovered that you can have active dreams, and that when you realize you are dreaming, you could control the dream.

I thought that was really amazing. I remember having a dream and saying to myself, "Okay, there's a bunch of books on the shelf. If I pull a book off the shelf and look at it, can I read the words in the book?" And I could, because your brain is making up the words in the book. Or you could be walking on a beach in your dream and pick up a handful of sand and you'd be looking at all the grains and thinking, "Well, my brain is putting all the millions of grains in this handful of sand."

What this immediately suggests—forgetting the alleged firewall between creation and perception in your brain—is the infinite potential of the human mind. To me, that is what is exciting. Because we talk about this all the time, using the analogy of the computer for the human brain. I am always interested by things that seem to defy that analogy. And I think dreaming...

JN: ... dreaming is a pretty good one.

CN: Yeah, because being able to create a whole world and to have a conversation with someone in a dream—you feel like you're having a conversation, but you're putting all the words into that other person's mouth.

JN: You're playing chess against yourself without realizing you're your own opponent.

CN: Yeah, which you can't do in waking life. There's no form of shadow boxing like that while you're awake.

JN: I think the first time I ever considered the fact that dreaming is different than perception was when you first described how sophisticated it is to me. It's a fascinating insight into what the mind is truly capable of because dreaming is so much bigger than perception. And yet it doesn't seem like there's a lot of critical scientific research being done on it.

CN: I would imagine dreaming doesn't attract a lot of scientific interest because of its subjectivity. It's so anecdotal.

JN: The subject has also been yoked into slightly bizarre and obsolete theories about psychology that have tainted it a bit. But none of those theories are really technical, although the mechanics of dreaming are incredible.

CN: Yeah, and I think it's possible to analyze those mechanics. It's when science and philosophy cross over, when this science of the human mind meets the philosophical edge, that I think people drift into abstraction. So what the film tries to do is keep it in the realm of science fiction—to keep it in the realm of the mechanical and the relatable so it doesn't become abstract and incomprehensible. There are rules to the way the characters use dreaming, which defines reality, which defines the dreams they enter. The characters take great pride in knowing these rules and that they apply absolutely.

JN: You get this great set of rules because the premise is that the dreamer can't know they're dreaming. You have to keep it bound. It's that much more exciting because it feels close to reality.

CN: I was definitely looking for a reason to impose rules in the story during the writing process. When I saw the first *Matrix* film, I thought it was really terrific, but I wasn't sure I quite understood the limits on the powers of the characters who had become self-aware.

Inception, on the other hand, is about a more everyday experience with dreaming. It's about a more relatable human experience. It doesn't question an actual reality. It's just saying, "Okay, we all dream every night. What if you could share your dream with someone else?" And it becomes an alternate reality simply because the dream becomes a form of communication—just like using a telephone or going online. I wanted it, then, to have a rule set, a set of reasons that you could graph for why it's not chaos and anarchy—for why it has to be order, and why you need architects and an architectural brain to create the world of the dream for the subject to enter.

JN: Everyone can be a Superman in their own dreams. But your protagonists approach the dream with expertise and subtlety—the subtlety of the way they manipulate the dream.

CN: Yes—exactly. It's about the subtlety and that is where the heist movie idea came from. I'd been dealing with the world of corporate espionage and so forth, but as soon as you want to present the subtle art of conning somebody, of fooling somebody, then you enter the world of the heist movie. And that is when I consider this script to have begun, when I figured out that I was going to use a heist movie structure to wrangle these ideas in, which was about ten years ago.

The problem I had was finishing it, because the heist movie as a genre tends to be deliberately superficial. It tends to be glamorous. It tends to be light entertainment. And I realized that when you're talking about dreaming, when you are talking about this universal human experience, you need the stakes of the story to have a much more emotional resonance. So the risk we're taking with genre in the case of *Inception*—rather than it being science fiction meets James Bond or whatever those sorts of things are—is saying, "Okay, we'll take a heist movie and we'll give it massive emotional stakes."

JN: In a funny way, it actually takes dreaming back to a kind of Freudian, Jungian place that speaks to how your innermost secrets are locked away in your dreams. So instead of stealing money or something superficial, you're actually stealing something very, very important. Or in this case, implanting something very, very important.

CN: Well, when you look at the world that the film suggests, your subconscious is going to start literally fortifying your secrets in the dreams. If you were in a dream-share and understand the rules of it, once your subconscious knows that it can create structures to defend itself or to protect information, then it's going to fortify naturally.

But also, in the way that our own minds are sort of treacherous, it's going to start leaking more and more secrets, and more and more things you're worried about, into that world. So it's this sort of weird escalation.

Think of Cobb, with his issues, as the onion of his character peels away during the film. And Ariadne, who is very much the person who pokes at that. The idea is that somebody who's really done a lot of this is going to be much stronger in the dream. But they're also going to be way more vulnerable, because their subconscious knows the stakes and knows all the things that can happen in this world. They're not innocent, in other words.

JN: Let's go back to the process of it. Ten years. What brought you back to the project?

CN: After I finish every film, I look at what I might do next. I would get the draft for *Inception* out and would read it, again. I would show it to Emma [Emma Thomas] and sometimes show it to you to get more thoughts on it. But I never quite knew how to finish it until I realized that the antagonist of the film should be the guy's wife.

JN: The antagonist had originally been his partner.

CN: Yes, it originally had been his partner. The heist movie conceit. His partner in crime, who had betrayed him and so forth. But that didn't lead anywhere emotionally. It didn't have any resonance. And as soon as it became his wife, that flipped the whole thing for me. That made it very, very relatable.

JN: Kind of unlocked the end of the film for you.

CN: It completely unlocked the end of the film. It completely unlocked how you could make something that a wider audience might care about. Because to me, whenever you deal in the world of esoteric or overly complex science fiction, or heist movies, or film noir, you're working for a smaller audience. If you're going to do a massive movie, though, you've got to be able to unlock that more universal experience for yourself as well as for the audience. That's what it took for me. As soon as I realized that Mal would be his wife, it became completely relatable.

JN: [*laughs*] Someone suggested to me—someone who had seen the film and admired it—that being married to one of your characters is a very, very bad idea. And when you tally it up, pretty much every film of yours has a dead wife in it. Dead wife. Dead girlfriend. Dead fiancée.

CN: I've written quite a few dead wives, that's true. But you try to put your relatable fears in these things. That's what film noir is, and I do view *Inception* as film noir. You take the things you are actually worried about in real life, or things you care about in real life, and you extrapolate that into a universal...

JN: ... domestic drama—painted as large as possible.

CN: You turn it into melodrama. People always talk about melodrama as a pejorative but I don't know what other word there is.

JN: It's fuel. That's why so many of these things always come back to it. And how it still manages to seem fresh each time. Hopefully.

CN: Well, yeah, hopefully.

JN: How about writing while you're directing? Is that tricky?

CN: I don't find it tricky because with everything I've worked on, whether I'm working on it with you or other writers (I worked with Hillary Seitz on *Insomnia*, for example), I've always taken it upon myself to do the last set of re-writes. And that lets me make it all go through the mill of my brain, my fingertips, my computer, whatever. And that allows me to feel as connected with it as stuff I've made up from nothing.

JN: But this one's all you. This is you carrying an idea for ten years. Is it different?

CN: No, it's no different to me than an adaptation. With *Memento*, for example, you gave me the short story, but from that point I was on my own in terms of feeling like, "Okay, now how do I make all that?" With *Inception*, while I came up with the concept myself, I started to take it for granted quite rapidly—almost like it was somebody else's thing. So it's not really that different.

The difference is that when you are working with your own idea, you are relying more on your own judgment for a much longer period of time. Whereas, when we write together, I'm looking at what you've done and then I'm—for a much shorter period of time—imposing my own judgments on that, and then getting it to you again. So there's this back and forth, and you deal with the idea intermittently for much shorter periods of time. When you're on your own for months and months and months, it's much harder to be objective about it.

And there's a lot of insecurity that comes with that. So when you put it out in the world and start to actually make the thing, there are definite moments. I had it with *Memento* and very much had it with *Inception*. We were checking prints, and I said to Jordan [Jordan Goldberg], about halfway through Reel 5, "I just suddenly realized: This is a really strange film—really strange!"

JN: But I do believe you've said that about most everything [*laughs*] we've worked on.

CN: Possibly, but with *The Dark Knight*, you see, I was able to look at the ferry scene at the end while mixing it, for example, and I'd say,

THE SHOOTING SCRIPT | 13

"Wow. This is a really unusual way to end a big action movie." But I already knew that because it was something you put in your draft, which made me immediately think, "I don't know about that." [*JN laughs*] I know that I spent months and months trying to see if that could change, but it couldn't.

JN: That's funny. We had the inverse relationship on *Batman Begins* with the microwave emitter, when you and David [David Goyer] came up with that. I sat there looking at it for a while [*CN laughs*] and finally said, "This is what it has to be."

CN: So when you're working with your own idea, on your own, there's no second-guessing in that sense. Second-guessing yourself is much harder than second-guessing other people. Much harder.

JN: I'm doing that right now on another project. It's a tricky one.

CN: It's very tricky.

JN: How about working with actors? This is a film where you've got some great actors, some great characters. How much work is required to bring those two things together?

CN: It's a great cast. I've been fortunate enough to work with great casts on all my films. Particularly with a lot of the smaller characters, the supporting characters, a great actor will come in with a whole take on it and they'll literally give what's on the page some kind of life that you hadn't foreseen. You're always in a much more intensive relationship with the protagonist since the truths of their character define where the narrative is going. Leo's [Leonardo DiCaprio] job on this film was very much the same as Guy Pearce's job on *Memento*. He had to open the sort of puzzle box emotionally for the audience and guide them through it. And Leo takes the truths of a characterization very seriously.

By far, the biggest burden on me as a screenwriter and director was during pre-production of the film, because I had to do an enormous amount of re-writing based on my conversations with Leo about Cobb. All of which I think was very productive for the movie, very essential to the movie. But I had to do that while I was prepping a film in six countries. Which was quite a big burden. But it had to be done, and I think we got it done very effectively.

I've had this with other actors—when they come in and they simply pull at why their character does particular things. Not in an abstract sense of "What's my motivation?," or whatever. They just sort of go, "Okay, I've walked in this door and I've walked up here and I say this. Why am I saying this? Why aren't I just going here?" And you have to actually think of it. And sometimes you have an answer. And sometimes you have an answer and they don't buy it. [*JN chuckles*] And other times you just don't have an answer and you know you've cheated on something and you've taken leaps. And certainly with Leo, you couldn't get by with any of the cheats, any of the situations where it's like, "I kind of know how to get from A to C through B, but not really." And so we put a lot of attention to working those things out. And I think we worked them out to my satisfaction, and hopefully to the audience's satisfaction, because that's really what the actor is helping you do at that point. They're sort of trying to be the conduit for the audience.

JN: They parse the film for the audience, as a proxy.

CN: Yeah.

JN: Well, that's a good segue to the next question I wanted to ask you, which is about the complexity of the film. This really, to me, feels like a marriage of all the different aspects of movies that I've seen you make: the sensibility of *Memento* and the complexity of that film, the interactivity of that film, the way that it asks the audience to work a little bit harder; and then the large-scale excitement and fun of something like *The Dark Knight*. This one really feels like you're using both skill sets. Did you ever think to yourself when you were working on the script, "Okay, no one's going to be able to follow me?" Is there a point of complexity where you feel like you hit your rev limiter and you don't want to go any further than that?

CN: There are points where you worry that you might be putting too much in and alienating the audience. But, funnily enough, some of those fears aren't correct. Sometimes, when you start thinking too much about what an audience is going to think, when you're too self-conscious about it, you make mistakes. Somewhere in the back of my mind, for example, I had assumed the business with the spinning top in the safe would wind up being cut out of the film. But when we started showing the film to people, that scene...

JN: You actually thought you'd have to cut it out?

CN: I thought we'd have to lose it because it was a symbol too far. Or an image too far. But what we realized in showing it to people is that they actually grasped the imagery as something to hold on to, as an illustration of things that had happened off camera.

JN: Right.

CN: So you can often misjudge that. The underlying philosophy for me, in terms of the complexity of the film, had always been that those things that had allowed *Memento* to succeed with audiences in a very mainstream fashion could be tapped to make a huge-scale movie. And that's the premise on which *Inception*'s been built. I tried to do it with my Howard Hughes project first. And when that wasn't going to fly, I put a lot of that thinking into this; into fusing the scale and entertainment value of a large film with something more—and I really don't want to say "challenging for an audience," because I don't think it is— that's just a little different and a little bit of a shift.

I had always felt that there was a big version of a film like *Memento* that could reach a wide audience, but the thing that gave me confidence in this idea was listening to how audiences reacted to *Memento* in a very mainstream way. Not by admiring it or finding it clever, but by just enjoying it. Guy Pearce was a huge part of that. Because I think I approached *Memento* in a quite cold manner. I approached it as a bit of a puzzle box. Casting an actor who looked for the emotional truth of the character and put it into every scene, though—that opened it up for an audience that never would have come to our film. And I learned from that. I learned that I had to trust Leo and his assessments of his character Cobb's truths. I also learned that in the script I had to pay attention to the feelings, to my emotional engagement with the material, insofar as I was standing in for the audience.

JN: There's a lovely moment close to the third act when Ellen Page as Ariadne makes a crack. You're rolling into the lowest level of the dream and she wonders whose dream we are in. And I remember watching the film for the first time with an audience and being struck with relief at that moment. It was like being let off the hook, as if the film was saying "Okay, this is a lot that's coming at you. But that's the point. It's fun." The complexity of it became part of the fun of it.

I think the proposition for you from *Memento* onwards, and I'm very much on board with this, is that the audience is not given enough credit—that people tend to think that there are very clear rules to what an audience can handle and what they can't handle. And this movie is a double barrel shotgun at those expectations.

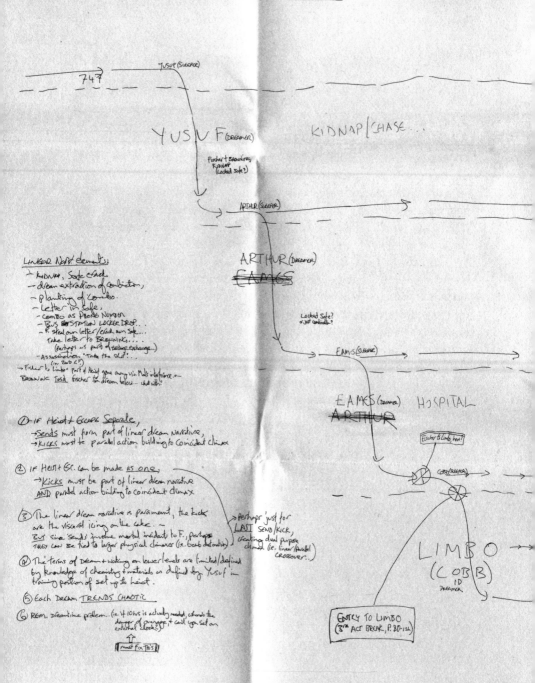

Nolan's graph detailing the team's path through the various layers
of the heist dream, and their subsequent "kick" back to reality.

ESCAP.6 (PARALLEL)

HOME

747

KICK   BRING F. ?

Potential Linear/Parallel
Crossover

YUSUF

SEND F.

KICK

EAMES

SEND F.

KICK

ARTHUR

SEND F.

SAITO (LIMBO)

TURN IN LIMBO

Shaded areas
are KEY climactic moment
for resolution of linear dream narrative,
ie. F. is there but must be sent on...

⇒ ie. action preceding this will not involve F.,
action post this F. will already be gone...

CN: Well, I've done really well so far in my career by trusting the audience to be as dissatisfied with convention as I am, as a filmgoer. You want to go see a film that surprises you in some way. Not for the sake of it, but because the people making the film are really trying to do something that they haven't seen a thousand times before themselves.

JN: Exactly.

CN: I give a film a lot of credit for trying to do something fresh—even if it doesn't work. You appreciate the effort, to a degree. I think the thing that I always react against as a filmgoer, though, is insincerity. That is to say, when somebody makes a film that they don't really enjoy themselves, just to produce an effect on the audience. And what really frustrates me with a film like *Inception* (or really anything that I've worked on) is when you show somebody the film and they think you're trying to be clever. Or show off. I always feel like I've completely failed at that point. Because I know as a filmgoer that's something I react against. Whether it's conventional or whether it's unconventional, you want to believe—you want to know—that the filmmaker loves the movie, loves what that movie does. That they love actually sitting there and watching that movie.

JN: Isn't that kind of the sad irony of making movies like this? Do you feel there's a little tinge of regret in the fact that you've written the script and made the movie, but that you will never really get to watch it? You end up making the movie you've always really wanted to see and then never really get to see it.

CN: I do get to see it. Because with every film there'll be one screening where, for whatever reason—because of who the audience is, or because of where I am technically in the process, or because of what elements I'm watching—I am actually able to watch the thing in a completely fresh way, like it isn't mine. And that's always a huge, huge pleasure. It's also a little frightening, and a little daunting, because you watch it in an incredibly heightened manner. And I think one of the reasons I still really love to screen the work print, cut it and tape it together, is that it's an incredibly stressful way of watching a film. Because the image is raw—it's not dressed up at all. It's an incredibly high-resolution image. But every splice can break, and the projector can bounce too much; you're terrified of the technical aspects for the audience. And that, in itself, makes you watch it in an incredibly attentive manner. You just see things and feel things you haven't felt while watching it on the Avid for months and months. It kind of reinvigorates the experience.

JN: When you describe the fragility of the work print, it occurs to me, drawing us back to the beginning of the conversation, that your job is an interesting one because you're not just watching the movie—you're creating the movie. You're not just experiencing reality—you're dreaming it for yourself. Did you think a lot about the connections to filmmaking and the dream-share technology in the film?

CN: You know, I never made that connection at all until you said it.

JN: [*laughs*] You're not supposed to let on about that.

CN: The heist movie aspects, too, closely parallel the process of making a film. You have a team of people working together. You've got a writer, you've got an actor, a production designer, a DP. But it had never occurred to me that everything I'm saying about creating a thing and trying to perceive it at the same time, which is what you're doing as you edit the film, relates absolutely to the filmmaking process. That's the whole thing you're trying to do: You're literally presenting this thing in which you've put words into people's mouths, and you're trying to watch it as if you're fresh to it.

JN: And the time shifting of it is similar because you get two years say, on average, to work on the projects you've done, and that's to create about two hours worth of perception. You can see, as you watch the film, how long it took you to shoot each individual moment, and it sort of congeals into something that suddenly goes by very quickly.

CN: But I would never want to make a film literally about filmmaking. But making something that you really relate to because of the work you do and the process you're engaged in, that's actually a lot of fun.

INCEPTION
THE SHOOTING SCRIPT

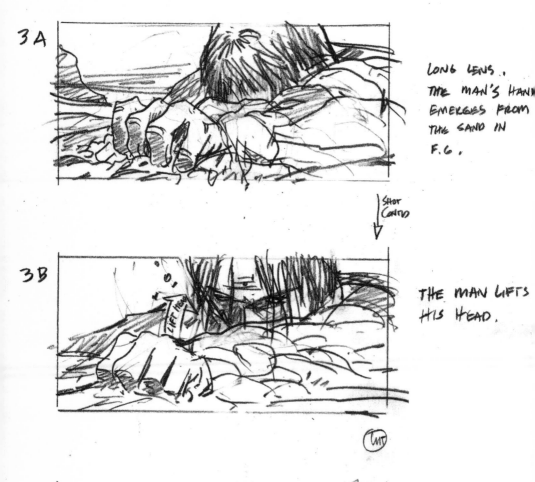

3 A

LONG LENS.
THE MAN'S HAND
EMERGES FROM
THE SAND IN
F.G.

Shot
Contd

3 B

THE MAN LIFTS
HIS HEAD.

CUT

4

A BLOND BOY
CROUCHES DOWN
THE BEACH NEXT
TO A SAND CASTLE

CUT

FADE IN:

DAWN. CRASHING SURF.

The waves TOSS a BEARDED MAN onto wet sand. He lies there.

A CHILD'S SHOUT makes him LIFT his head to see: a LITTLE BLONDE BOY crouching, back towards us, watching the tide eat a SANDCASTLE. A LITTLE BLONDE GIRL joins the boy. The Bearded Man tries to call to them, but they RUN OFF, FACES UNSEEN. He COLLAPSES.

The barrel of a rifle ROLLS the Bearded Man onto his back. A JAPANESE SECURITY GUARD looks down at him, then calls up the beach to a colleague leaning against a JEEP. Behind them is a cliff, and on top of that, a JAPANESE CASTLE.

INT. ELEGANT DINING ROOM, JAPANESE CASTLE—LATER

The Security Guard waits as an ATTENDANT speaks to an ELDERLY JAPANESE MAN sitting at the dining table, back to us.

> ### ATTENDANT
> (in Japanese)
> He was delirious. But asked for you by name.
> And...
> (to the Security Guard)
> Show him.

> ### SECURITY GUARD
> (in Japanese)
> He was carrying nothing but this...

He puts a HANDGUN on the table. The Elderly Man keeps eating.

> ### SECURITY GUARD
> ...and this.

The Security Guard places a SMALL PEWTER CONE alongside the gun. The Elderly Man STOPS eating. Picks up the cone.

> ### ELDERLY JAPANESE MAN
> (in Japanese)
> Bring him here. And some food.

INT. SAME—MOMENTS LATER

The Elderly Japanese Man watches the Bearded Man WOLF down his food. He SLIDES the handgun down the table towards him.

> ELDERLY JAPANESE MAN
> (in English)
> Are you here to kill me?

The Bearded Man glances up at him, then back to his food.

The Elderly Japanese Man picks up the cone between thumb and forefinger.

> ELDERLY JAPANESE MAN
> I know what *this* is.

He SPINS it onto the table— it CIRCLES gracefully across the polished ebony... a SPINNING TOP.

> ELDERLY JAPANESE MAN
> I've seen one before. Many, many years ago...

The Elderly Japanese Man STARES at the top, mesmerized.

> ELDERLY JAPANESE MAN
> It belonged to a man I met in a half-remembered dream...

MOVE IN on the GRACEFULLY SPINNING TOP...

> ELDERLY JAPANESE MAN
> A man possessed of some radical notions...

The Elderly Japanese Man STARES, remembering...

> COBB (V.O.)
> *What's the most resilient parasite?*

CUT TO:

INT. SAME ELEGANT DINING ROOM—NIGHT (YEARS EARLIER)

The speaker, COBB, is 35, handsome, tailored. A young Japanese man, SAITO, eats as he listens.

> COBB

A bacteria? A virus?

Cobb gestures at their feast with his wine glass–

> COBB

An intestinal worm?

Saito's fork pauses, mid-air. Cobb GRINS. A third man is at the table–
ARTHUR. He jumps in to save the pitch–

> ARTHUR

What Mr. Cobb is trying to say—

> COBB

An *idea*.

Saito looks at Cobb, curious.

> COBB

Resilient, highly contagious. Once an idea's
taken hold in the brain it's almost impossible to
eradicate. A person can cover it up, ignore it—
but it stays there.

> SAITO

But surely—to forget...?

> COBB

Information, yes. But an *idea*? Fully formed,
understood? That sticks...
> (taps forehead)
In there, somewhere.

> SAITO

For someone like you to steal?

> ARTHUR

Yes. In the dream state, conscious defenses are
lowered and your thoughts become vulnerable
to theft. It's called extraction.

> COBB

But, Mr. Saito, we can train your subconscious
to defend itself from even the most skilled
extractor.

                          SAITO
          How can you do that?

                          COBB
          Because I *am* the most skilled extractor. I know
          how to search your mind and find your secrets.
          I know the tricks, and I can teach them to your
          subconscious so that even when you're *asleep*,
          your guard is never down.

Cobb leans forwards, holding Saito's gaze.

                          COBB
          But if I'm going to help you, you have to be
          completely open with me. I'll need to know my
          way around your thoughts better than your wife,
          your analyst, anyone.
                     (gestures around)
          If this is a dream and you've got a safe full of
          secrets, I need to know what's in that safe. For
          this to work, you have to let me in.

Saito gives this a flicker of a smile. Rises. A BODYGUARD opens double
doors which give onto a LAVISH PARTY.

                          SAITO
          Gentlemen. Enjoy your evening as I consider
          your proposal.

They watch Saito leave. Arthur turns to Cobb, worried–

                         ARTHUR
          He knows.

Cobb motions silence. A TREMOR starts, they steady their glasses, Cobb
glances at his watch– THE SECOND HAND IS FROZEN.

                         ARTHUR
          What's going on up there?

And we–

CUT TO:

INT. FILTHY BATHROOM—DAY (FEELS LIKE DIFFERENT TIME)

Cobb, ASLEEP, SITTING IN A CHAIR AT THE END OF A STEAMING BATH. The chair is up on a cabinet- the bottom of the legs level with the rim of the tub.

A sweating man (40's) watches over Cobb. This is NASH. A distant EXPLOSION rumbles through the room. Nash moves to the window, parts the curtains. Outside: a CHAOTIC DEVELOPING-WORLD CITY- the street filled with RIOTERS- SMASHING, BURNING.

Nash checks Cobb's left wrist: above his watch, tape holds TWO THIN YELLOW TUBES in place. Nash looks at Cobb's watch- THE SECOND HAND CRAWLS UNNATURALLY SLOWLY.

Nash follows the tubes to a SILVER BRIEFCASE at Arthur's feet: ARTHUR IS ASLEEP in an armchair. Tubes connect the briefcase to Arthur's wrist.

Nash follows another set of tubes from the briefcase to where they pass under the door to the bedroom. Through the crack of the door, Nash sees SAITO ASLEEP on the bed, tubes running to his wrist. BOOM- a closer EXPLOSION, and we–

CUT TO:

INT. BULLET TRAIN COMPARTMENT—DAY (FEELS LIKE DIFFERENT TIME)

Nash, ASLEEP. Head ROCKING AGAINST THE WINDOW as the train BUMPS OVER A ROUGH PIECE OF TRACK.

A Japanese Man, TODASHI (18) watches Nash nervously. He checks Nash's wrist: TWO YELLOW TUBES CONNECT NASH WITH THREE OTHER SLEEPING MEN IN THE COMPARTMENT: COBB, ARTHUR, SAITO.

Todashi checks his watch: THE SECOND HAND TICKS IN REAL TIME. Another TRAIN PASSES in the opposite direction with a MIGHTY WHUMP- Todashi's eyes FLY to Nash's sleeping face–

NASH JERKS WITH THE MOVEMENT OF THE TRAIN, and we–

CUT TO:

INT. FILTHY BATHROOM—CONTINUOUS

Another EXPLOSION– Nash CHECKS the sleeping Cobb and we–

CUT TO:

EXT. ROOFTOP TERRACES, JAPANESE CASTLE—NIGHT

A LOW TREMOR RUMBLES THROUGH THE CASTLE. Cobb and Arthur steady themselves against the wooden rail. Several TILES and pieces of MASONRY fall. Below them a BLACK SEA churns. Other GUESTS wander the massive terraces.

> ARTHUR
> Saito *knows*. He's playing with us.

> COBB
> I can get it here. The information's in the safe—
> he looked right at it when I mentioned secrets.

Arthur nods. Then spots someone over Cobb's shoulder.

> ARTHUR
> What's *she* doing here, Cobb?

Cobb turns to see a beautiful woman, elegantly dressed, staring out at the sea. This is MAL. Cobb watches her.

> COBB
> You just get to your room. I'll take care of the
> rest.

> ARTHUR
> See that you do. We're here to work.

Arthur brushes past Mal, shaking his head. She nears Cobb. Looks out at the DROP. The WIND WHIPS HER HAIR–

> MAL
> If I jumped, would I survive?

> COBB
> With a clean dive, perhaps. Mal, why are you
> here?

She turns to look at him. Amused.

> MAL
>
> I thought you might be missing me...

She smiles. He leans in, mesmerized.

> COBB
>
> I am. But I can't trust you anymore.

She stares up at him, inviting.

> MAL
>
> So what?

INT. BEDROOM SUITE, JAPANESE CASTLE—MOMENTS LATER

Mal sips champagne as she studies a painting by Francis Bacon.

> MAL
>
> Looks like Arthur's taste.

Cobb is looking down through the window at the GUARDS patrolling the castle at ground level.

> COBB
>
> Actually, Mr. Saito is partial to postwar British painters.

He turns to Mal, donning a pair of black leather gloves.

> COBB
>
> Would you sit down?

Mal lowers herself gracefully into a leather wingback chair. Cobb approaches, pulls out a length of BLACK ROPE and kneels at Mal's feet. She looks down at him.

> MAL
>
> Tell me...

Cobb TIES the rope around the CHAIR LEGS.

> MAL
>
> Do the children miss me?

Cobb pauses. He lets his gloved fingers lightly touch Mal's ankle. He looks up at her.

> COBB
>
> You can't imagine.

Mal looks away, uncomfortable. Cobb gets to his feet, letting out the rope as he moves back to the window.

> MAL
>
> What're you doing?

Cobb tosses the rope out–

> COBB
>
> Getting some air.

He tugs on the rope, testing. The weight of the chair, with Mal on it, holds.

> COBB
>
> Stay seated. Please.

And with that, he JUMPS. Mal considers the open window.

EXT. JAPANESE CASTLE WALL—CONTINUOUS

Cobb RAPPELS down the wall, darting past windows. He stops at a particular one. Gets out a glass cutter–

Suddenly he starts DROPPING–

INT. BEDROOM SUITE, JAPANESE CASTLE—CONTINUOUS

The EMPTY CHAIR SLIDES across the floor– WEDGES under the window–

EXT. JAPANESE CASTLE WALL—CONTINUOUS

Cobb JOLTS to a stop 15 ft. lower. He looks up at the bedroom window. Shakes his head. Starts climbing back.

INT. KITCHEN, JAPANESE CASTLE—MOMENTS LATER

Cobb drops silently from the window into the darkened kitchen. He pulls a PISTOL from his belt, screwing a SILENCER onto the barrel as he GLIDES across the room.

INT. HALL, JAPANESE CASTLE—CONTINUOUS

Cobb SLIPS through the shadows towards a GUARD stationed at the head of a GRAND STAIRCASE...

The Guard HEARS something– TURNS– PEERS into the shadows...

Cobb FLASHES out of the shadows, silenced pistol up, AIMING–

PHHT– head shot– the Guard starts to drop... but Cobb is already there to CATCH him, sliding on his knees and lowering the Guard SILENTLY to the floor.

INT. DINING ROOM, JAPANESE CASTLE—CONTINUOUS

Cobb moves to a PAINTING. With practiced hands he removes it from the wall, revealing a SAFE. Cobb spins the dial, pulls it OPEN, GRABS an envelope from within, stuffs it into his waistband, where there is already an IDENTICAL ENVELOPE.

THE LIGHTS COME ON. Cobb freezes.

> SAITO (O.S.)
> Turn around.

Cobb turns. At the far end of the room: Saito. Next to him is Mal, gun in hand. She smiles at Cobb.

> MAL
> The gun, Dom.

Cobb doesn't move. Mal motions outside– two GUARDS drag Arthur into the room. Mal puts the gun to his head.

> MAL
> Please.

Cobb slowly places his gun at his end of the long table, then SLIDES it along the polished ebony. It comes to rest HALFWAY down the length of the table.

> SAITO
> Now the envelope, Mr. Cobb.

Cobb reaches into his waistband, removes ONE of the envelopes, SLIDES it along the table. Steps back, hands raised.

COBB

Did *she* tell you, or have you known all along?

SAITO

That you're here to steal from me?
(beat)
Or that we're actually asleep?

Arthur gives Cobb an I-told-you-so look.

SAITO

I want to know who your employer is.

Mal COCKS the gun at Arthur's temple.

COBB

No point threatening him in a dream.

MAL

That depends on what you're threatening.
Killing him would just wake him up... but pain?
Pain is in the mind...

Mal LOWERS the gun and SHOOTS Arthur in the leg– Arthur drops, SCREAMING– Mal looks at Cobb, cold.

MAL

And, judging by the decor, we're in *your* mind,
aren't we, Arthur?

Cobb watches Arthur's PAIN. Mal aims at Arthur's other leg...

Cobb SPRINGS for the table, SKIDDING along its polished surface– he GRABS his gun– SHOOTS ARTHUR BETWEEN THE EYES–

Arthur DROPS– the room starts to SHUDDER in a MASSIVE EARTHQUAKE– Cobb SPRINGS for the door– Arthur's eyes stare at the ceiling, DEAD, and we–

CUT TO:

INT. FILTHY BATHROOM—DAY

Arthur's EYES OPEN as he WAKES IN THE ARMCHAIR– he GRABS at the tubes at his wrist, YANKING them free–

HE SLIDES
THE ENVELOPE.

COCKS GUN

SHE SHOOTS ARTHUR
IN THE LEG ..

15-16B

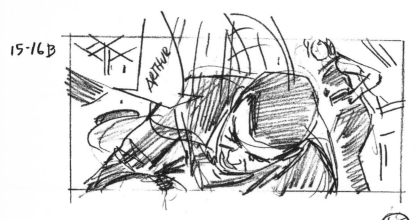

ARTHUR FALLS
TO LENS ..

15-17

SHE POINTS THE
GUN AT HIS
OTHER LEG .

15-18

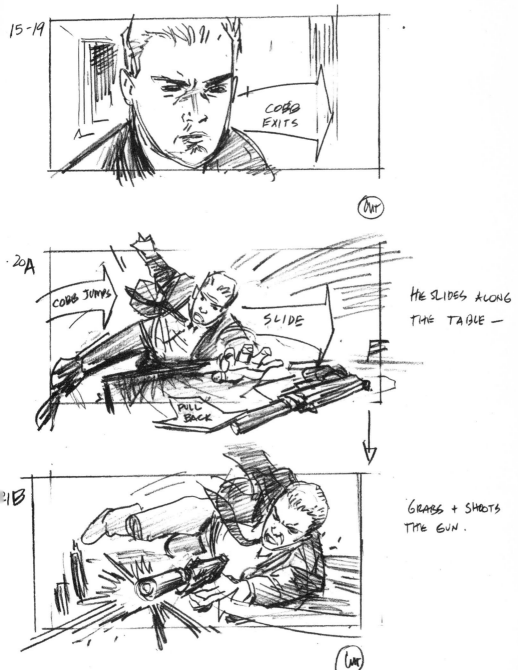

15-19

COBB EXITS

CUT

20A

COBB JUMPS

SLIDE

PULL BACK

HE SLIDES ALONG THE TABLE —

21B

GRABS + SHOOTS THE GUN.

CUT

15-22

ARTHUR SHOT
BETWEEN THE
EYES.

(CUT)

15-23

THE ROOM ST
TO SHUDDE

(CUT)

15-24

WIDE —
A MASSIVE
EARTHQUAK

(CUT)

-25A

COBB SPRINGS
FOR THE DOOR.

COBB

SHOT
CONT'D

-25B

EXITS.

EXIT

5-26

ARTHUR'S EYES
STARE AT THE
CEILING ..

SCENE # 16

16-1 A

TILT DOWN

SHOT CONT'D

INT. DIRTY
BATHROOM:
ARTHER'S EYE
SNAP OPEN.
TILT DOWN

16-1B

CUT

HE YANKS FR
THE TUBES.

16-2A

ARTHUR

TILT DOWN

SHOT CONT'D

NASH

"WHAT'RE YOU
DOING? IT'S
TOO SOON —"

16-2B

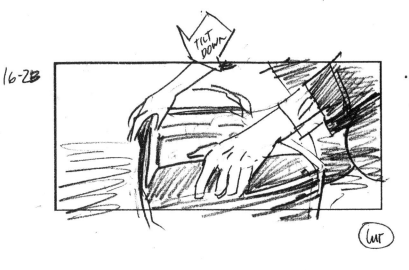

TILT DOWN

ARTHUR GRABS CASE,

(CUT)

16-2C

ARTHUR

RUNS TO THE DOOR.

SHOT CONT'D

16-2D

OPENS IT...

SHOT CONT'D

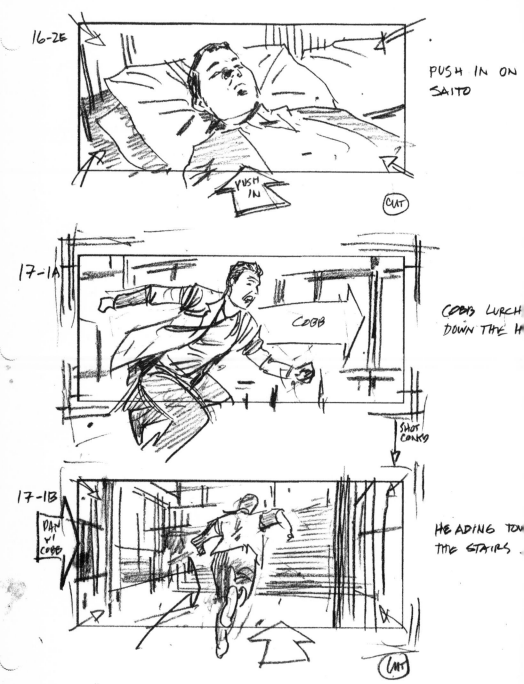

16-2E

PUSH IN ON
SAITO

PUSH
IN

CUT

17-1A

COBB

COB'S LURCH
DOWN THE H

SHOT
CONT'S

17-1B

DAN
V
COBB

HEADING TOW
THE STAIRS

CUT

> NASH
>
> What're you doing?! It's too soon—

FLUID spurts from the tubes as Arthur STRUGGLES with the SILVER CASE on the bathroom floor.

> ARTHUR
>
> I know! We have to reconnect the loop before
> they wake up!

Arthur grabs the case and pushes through the door to the bedroom—following the tubes to where they meet Saito's wrist— SAITO LIES ON THE BED, ASLEEP. Saito STIRS and we—

CUT TO:

INT. JAPANESE CASTLE CORRIDOR—NIGHT

Cobb LURCHES towards the stairs, as all around him the building BUCKS and HEAVES—

INT. DINING ROOM, JAPANESE CASTLE—CONTINUOUS

Saito and the Guards PANIC. Mal walks calmly through the destruction, picks up the envelope and turns to Saito.

> MAL
>
> He was close. Very close.

EXT. GRAND STAIRCASE, JAPANESE CASTLE—CONTINUOUS

Cobb runs up the stairs, pulling out the SECOND ENVELOPE—

INT. DINING ROOM, JAPANESE CASTLE—CONTINUOUS

Saito RIPS open the envelope, pulls out sheets of paper. He looks at Mal, PANICKED. He turns to the Guards—

> SAITO
>
> Stop him!

Mal, confused, looks at the sheets of paper: THEY ARE BLANK. Mal smiles, amused.

INT. GRAND STAIRCASE, JAPANESE CASTLE—CONTINUOUS

As Cobb runs up the stairs he reads the TYPEWRITTEN SHEETS from his envelope, and we–

CUT TO:

INT. DILAPIDATED HOTEL ROOM—DAY

Arthur OPENS the silver case: a COMPLEX MECHANISM of TUBES, SYRINGES, DOSAGE CONTROLLERS. Arthur's hands fly across the machine's controls as he glances at Saito's STIRRING face–

ARTHUR
I'm not going to make it! Wake Cobb!

INT. FILTHY BATHROOM—CONTINUOUS

Nash turns to Cobb. Raises his hand and SMACKS him across the face, and we–

CUT TO:

INT. GRAND STAIRCASE, JAPANESE CASTLE—NIGHT

Cobb is SMASHED sideways off his feet...

INT. DINING ROOM, JAPANESE CASTLE—NIGHT

The CEILING CRACKS above Saito– he looks up as a TON of STONE floods down, CRUSHING HIM and we–

CUT TO:

INT. DILAPIDATED HOTEL ROOM—DAY

Saito's eyes FLICKER OPEN. AWAKE.

INT. FILTHY BATHROOM—CONTINUOUS

Nash SMACKS Cobb again–

NASH
He won't wake!

INT. DILAPIDATED HOTEL ROOM—CONTINUOUS

Arthur, crouched by Saito, connects the second tube.

> ARTHUR
> Dunk him!

A CLICK: Arthur looks up to find Saito with a gun to his head and a finger to his lips, gesturing silence...

INT. FILTHY BATHROOM—CONTINUOUS

Nash puts his hand on Cobb's forehead and PUSHES HIM BACKWARDS— as Cobb starts to FALL BACKWARDS in the chair we are in SLOW MOTION, and we—

> CUT TO:

INT. GRAND STAIRCASE, JAPANESE CASTLE—NIGHT

Cobb, full speed, picks himself up, scrambling to read the last sheet of paper. He stares at it PUZZLED— bullets hit around him as the Guards race up the stairs and we—

> CUT TO:

INT. FILTHY BATHROOM—DAY

Cobb, in SLOW MOTION, hits the WATER— head THRASHING as he goes under— and we—

> CUT TO:

INT. GRAND STAIRCASE, JAPANESE CASTLE—NIGHT

Cobb glances up from the paper as WATER EXPLODES IN THROUGH ALL THE WINDOWS, FLOODING THE ENTIRE HALL—

COBB IS SWAMPED BY WATER, SPUN IN ALL DIRECTIONS AT ONCE— HE PULLS DEEPER OR FOR THE SURFACE, WE CAN'T TELL...

HE BREAKS THE SURFACE, GASPING FOR AIR IN THE BATHTUB IN THE—

INT. FILTHY BATHROOM—DAY

Cobb's AWAKE, GULPING AIR, getting his bearings.

Saito SMASHES into the room, KNOCKING Nash down- Cobb LAUNCHES himself out of the tub, FLYING dripping wet across the room to SLAM Saito against the door- the gun DROPS, Cobb's fist CONNECTS with Saito's jaw and the struggle is over.

INT. DILAPIDATED HOTEL ROOM—MOMENTS LATER

Cobb, wet but composed, sits, turning Saito's gun in his hand. Nash holds Saito's arms behind him. Outside, the sounds of RIOTING grow louder.

> COBB
>
> You came prepared.

> SAITO
>
> I bring the gun because not even my head of security knows this apartment. How did *you* find it?

Arthur, at the window, looks out at the WORSENING VIOLENCE.

> COBB
>
> Hard for a man in your position to keep a love nest totally secret... particularly when there's a married woman involved.

> SAITO
>
> She would never...

> COBB
>
> And yet, here we are.

Saito is silent.

> COBB
>
> With a dilemma.

> SAITO
>
> You got what you came for.

> COBB
>
> Not quite. The key piece of information wasn't there, was it, Mr. Saito?

Arthur looks over at Cobb, worried.

> ARTHUR
> They're getting closer, Cobb.

And we–

CUT TO:

INT. BULLET TRAIN COMPARTMENT—DAY

Todashi slips a pair of HEADPHONES over Nash's ears, then pulls out an MP3 player and we–

CUT TO:

INT. DILAPIDATED HOTEL ROOM—DAY

Saito's eyes are on the floor.

> COBB
> You held something back because you knew
> what we were up to...

Cobb uses the barrel of the gun to raise Saito's chin.

> COBB
> So why let us in at all?

Saito smiles, defiant. VIOLENT NOISES echo up the stairway...

> SAITO
> An audition.

> COBB
> Audition for what?

> SAITO
> It doesn't matter. You failed.

> COBB
> I extracted all the information you had in there.

> SAITO
> But your deception was readily apparent.

And we–

CUT TO:

INT. BULLET TRAIN COMPARTMENT—DAY

Todashi opens the SILVER BRIEFCASE, revealing the complex mechanism of syringes and controllers– FOUR CONTROLLERS DISPLAY COUNTDOWNS.

Todashi waits for the first countdown to hit "30," then HITS PLAY on the MP3 player– He watches Nash's sleeping face as he RAISES the volume...

Through Nash's headphones: the opening bars of Edith Piaf's "Non, je ne regrette rien," and we–

CUT TO:

INT. DILAPIDATED HOTEL ROOM—DAY

In the distant background, strange MASSIVE low-end MUSICAL TONES start, sounding like DISTANT HORNS...

> SAITO
>
> So leave me and go.

> COBB
>
> You know the corporation who hired us won't
> accept failure. We won't last two days...

The DISTANT, SLOWED-DOWN MUSIC is becoming LOUDER, as are the SHOUTS coming up the stairs. Arthur looks at his watch, its SLOW SECOND TICKING MARKS TIME WITH THE MASSIVE MUSIC.

> ARTHUR
>
> Come on, Cobb.

> COBB
>
> So now I have to do this the old-fashioned way—

Cobb GRABS SAITO AND PUTS HIS HEAD TO THE FLOOR, gun pressed into his cheek. Saito looks into Cobb's eyes– sees he *will* pull the trigger. Saito BLINKS, looks away in shame–

When he NOTICES SOMETHING. And starts LAUGHING.

SAITO

I've always hated this carpet.

Cobb's eyes flick to the carpet and back.

SAITO

It's stained and frayed in such distinctive ways...

Cobb looks up at Nash, who shrugs, at a loss.

SAITO

But very definitely made of *wool*. Right now I'm
lying on polyester.

Cobb glares at Nash, and we–

CUT TO:

INT. BULLET TRAIN COMPARTMENT—DAY

Todashi watches the first of the countdowns hit ZERO– He looks up at
Arthur, STIRRING, and we–

CUT TO:

INT. DILAPIDATED HOTEL ROOM—DAY

Saito turns from the carpet to look up at Cobb.

SAITO

Which means I'm not lying on *my* carpet, in *my*
apartment...
(smiles)
You've lived up to your reputation, Mr. Cobb...
I'm still dreaming.

Cobb looks over to Arthur, but ARTHUR HAS VANISHED, and we–

CUT TO:

INT. BULLET TRAIN COMPARTMENT—DAY

Arthur's eyes flicker open, AWAKE. He RIPS at his tubes.

TODASHI

How'd it go?

> ARTHUR
>
> Not good.

Arthur checks the remaining three countdowns, and we–

CUT TO:

INT. DILAPIDATED HOTEL ROOM—DAY

Saito gets to his feet, looking admiringly at Cobb.

> SAITO
>
> A dream within a dream—I'm impressed.

Cobb lowers the gun. Defeated. Glances at his watch. The music REVER-BERATES, the RIOTERS BANG ON THE DOOR, and we–

CUT TO:

INT. BULLET TRAIN COMPARTMENT—DAY

Arthur retracts the tubes into the case as he watches the next count-down hit ZERO, and we–

CUT TO:

INT. DILAPIDATED HOTEL ROOM—DAY

Another BANG on the door– Saito, confident now, approaches Cobb. Nash is behind Saito.

> SAITO
>
> But in my dream, we really ought to be playing
> by my rules...

> NASH
>
> Ah, yes, but you see, Mr. Saito—

Saito turns to Nash–

> COBB
>
> We're not in *your* dream—

Saito turns back to Cobb, BUT COBB HAS VANISHED–

> NASH
>
> We're in mine.

Saito SPINS back to Nash– the DOOR SMASHES OFF ITS HINGES AS RIOT-ERS POUR INTO THE ROOM, SWARMING OVER NASH... BUT NASH IS GONE. The music DIES. Saito and the rioters stand there in the SILENCE, the light DWINDLING... and we–

CUT TO:

INT. BULLET TRAIN COMPARTMENT—DAY

Nash's eyes open, AWAKE.

> ARTHUR (O.S.)
> Asshole!

Nash BLINKS. Arthur is in his face, furious.

> ARTHUR
> How could you get the carpet wrong?!

> NASH
> It wasn't my fault!

> ARTHUR
> You're the *architect*—

> NASH
> I didn't know he was going to rub his damn cheek on it!

Cobb PULLS Arthur away from Nash.

> COBB
> Let's go.

> ARTHUR
> And you—what the hell was all that?

> COBB
> I had it under control.

> ARTHUR
> I'd hate to see out of control—

> COBB
> There's no time for this—I'm getting off at Kyoto.

>   ARTHUR
>
> Why? He's not gonna search every compart-
> ment.

>   COBB
>
> I can't stand trains.

Arthur moves to the briefcase. Turns a dial.

>   ARTHUR
>
> I can keep him under for one minute—

Arthur hits a button— A PLUNGER DEPRESSES. Cobb RIPS the tape off
Saito's wrist, ROLLS up his tubes. Arthur SLAMS the silver case shut.
Todashi pulls open the door–

>   COBB
>
> Every man for himself.

Arthur and Nash EXIT, heading in different directions down the corridor. Cobb hands Todashi a thick roll of CASH, looks at Saito, who STIRS.
Cobb moves off.

EXT. JAPANESE COUNTRYSIDE—CONTINUOUS

The BULLET TRAIN speeds through the lush landscape.

INT. BULLET TRAIN COMPARTMENT—CONTINUOUS

Saito WAKES GENTLY. Looks around the compartment, empty but for
Todashi, reading a comic. Saito looks down at his wrist. Sees a small
mark. Rubs it. SMILES.

EXT. TOKYO—DUSK

Moving over the vast city towards a high rise. A HELICOPTER thumps
into frame, heading for a pad on the roof.

INT. APARTMENT, TOKYO—CONTINUOUS

Cobb sits, waiting. Checks his watch, restless. He pulls a HANDGUN.
Checks it is loaded. Places it on the table in front of him. Pulls out a
PEWTER SPINNING TOP, SPINS it on the table... He INTENTLY STUDIES
the top's spin... As he stares, the sound of a FREIGHT TRAIN builds and
builds– the top WOBBLES, TIPS onto its side– the sound of the train
STOPS. the PHONE RINGS– Cobb GRABS it–

> CHILDREN'S VOICES (over phone)
> *Hi, Daddy! Hi, Dad.*

> COBB
> Hey, guys. How are you?

> CHILDREN'S VOICES (over phone)
> *Good. Okay, I guess.*

Cobb closes his eyes, trying to picture his children: INSERT CUT: COBB'S MEMORY– a LITTLE BLONDE BOY (3), *back towards us, crouches* IN A GARDEN, *looks at something in the grass...*

> COBB
> Who's just okay? Was that James?

> JAMES (over phone)
> *Yeah. When are you coming home?*

> COBB
> I can't. Not for a while.

INSERT CUT: A LITTLE BLONDE GIRL (5), *also* FACE UNSEEN, *joins* JAMES, CROUCHING BESIDE HIM...

> JAMES (over phone)
> *Why?*

> COBB
> Well, James, like I've told you—I'm away
> because I'm working...

> LITTLE GIRL (over phone)
> *Grandma says you're never coming back.*

Cobb pauses. Takes a breath. INSERT CUT: James and Philippa, FACES UNSEEN, *lift their heads from the grass, responding to someone's call–they* RUN AWAY FROM US ACROSS THE GARDEN...

> COBB
> Philippa, can you ask Grandma to pick up the
> phone—

> PHILIPPA (over phone)
> *She's shaking her head.*

Cobb TENSES, as if about to SMASH the phone.

> COBB
>
> Well, we'll just have to hope Grandma's wrong about that won't we?

> JAMES (over phone)
>
> *Daddy?*

> COBB
>
> Yes?

> JAMES (over phone)
>
> *Is Mommy with you?*

Cobb looks like he just got punched– INSERT CUT: COBB'S MEMORY– MAL, WIND BLOWING HER HAIR, SMILES CALMLY...

> COBB
>
> No. No, we talked about this, James. Mommy's gone.

> JAMES (over phone)
>
> Where?

> GRANDMA'S VOICE (over phone)
>
> *Time to go, kids. Say bye-bye—*

> COBB
>
> I'll give some presents to Grandpa, okay? Just be good for—

Cobb STARES at the dead phone. Then DOWNS his drink– A KNOCK at the door. Cobb GRABS the top, the gun– MOVES to the door– cracks it: Arthur.

> ARTHUR
>
> Our ride's on the roof.

Cobb nods. Moves to pick up his bag. Arthur watches.

> ARTHUR
>
> Cobb... are you okay?

Cobb looks up.

> COBB

Yeah, why?

> ARTHUR

Down in the dream... Mal showing up like that...

> COBB

Yeah. I'm sorry about your leg.

> ARTHUR

It's getting worse, isn't it?

> COBB

One apology's all you're getting, Arthur. Now, where's Nash?

> ARTHUR

Hasn't shown. Wanna wait?

> COBB
> (shakes head)

We were supposed to deliver Saito's expansion plans to Cobol Engineering two hours ago. By now they know we failed. Time to disappear.

INT. CORRIDOR—CONTINUOUS

Cobb and Arthur head towards the elevator.

> ARTHUR

Where will you go?

> COBB

Buenos Aires. I can lie low there. Maybe sniff out a job when things quiet down. You?

> ARTHUR

Stateside.

> COBB
> (wistful)

'Course. Send my regards.

Arthur looks at Cobb. Nods. Sympathetic.

EXT. ROOFTOP HELIPAD—NIGHT

The HELICOPTER sits, ROTORS SPINNING. As Cobb and Arthur reach the door, it SLIDES OPEN. Cobb steps up into the leather-padded interior. He freezes.

INT. HELICOPTER ON PAD—CONTINUOUS

Nash, BEATEN BLOODY, sits on the far side, slumped against the window. Beside him: SAITO. He nods politely at Cobb.

> SAITO
> He sold you out. Thought to come to me and bargain for his life...

Saito's BODYGUARD offers Cobb a GUN.

> SAITO
> So I offer you the satisfaction.

> COBB
> That's not how I deal with things.

> SAITO
> Would you work with him again?

Cobb shakes his head. Saito's BODYGUARDS PULL Nash from the chopper. Saito motions Cobb and Arthur to sit. The chopper RISES. Cobb watches Nash DRAGGED across the pad.

> COBB
> What will you do to him?

> SAITO
> Nothing. But I can't speak for your friends from Cobol Engineering.

Saito looks out at the city slipping by.

> COBB
> What do you want from us?

> SAITO
> Inception.

Arthur raises his eyebrows. Cobb is poker-faced.

> SAITO

Is it possible?

> ARTHUR

Of course not.

> SAITO

If you can steal an idea from someone's mind, why can't you plant one there instead?

> ARTHUR

Okay, here's planting an idea: I say to you, "Don't think about elephants."
>> (Saito nods)
What are you thinking about?

> SAITO

Elephants.

> ARTHUR

Right. But it's not *your* idea because you know I gave it to you.

> SAITO

You could plant it *subconsciously*—

> ARTHUR

The subject's mind can always trace the genesis of the idea. True inspiration is impossible to fake.

> COBB

No, it isn't.

> SAITO

Can you do it?

> COBB

I won't do it.

> SAITO

In exchange, I'll give you the information you were paid to steal.

                         COBB

Are you giving me a choice? Because I can find
my own way to square things with Cobol.

                         SAITO

Then you do have a choice.

                         COBB

And I choose to leave.

EXT. AIRFIELD—MOMENTS LATER

The helicopter sets down next to a PRIVATE JET.

INT. HELICOPTER—CONTINUOUS

Saito indicates the plane.

                         SAITO

Tell the crew where you want to go, they'll file
the plan en route.

Cobb and Arthur look at each other. Then move for the door.

                         SAITO

Mr. Cobb...? There is one other thing I could
offer you.
                    (Cobb stops)
How would you like to go home? To America.
To your children.

Cobb turns back to Saito.

                         COBB

You can't fix that. Nobody could.

                         SAITO

Just like inception.

Cobb considers this. Arthur touches his arm.

                         ARTHUR

Cobb, come on—

                         COBB

How complex is the idea?

                    SAITO
Simple enough.

                    COBB
No idea's simple when you have to plant it in
someone else's mind.

                    SAITO
My main competitor is an old man in poor
health. His son will soon inherit control of the
corporation. I need him to decide to break up
his father's empire. Against his own self-interest.

                    ARTHUR
Cobb, we should walk away from this.

                    COBB
If I were to do it. If I *could* do it... how do I know
you can deliver?

                    SAITO
You don't. But I can. So do you want to take a
leap of faith, or become an old man, filled with
regret, waiting to die alone?

Cobb looks at Saito. Barely nods.

                    SAITO
Assemble your team, Mr. Cobb. And choose
your people more wisely.

INT. PRIVATE JET—LATER

Cobb reclines his seat. Arthur picks at a salad, angry.

                    ARTHUR
I know how much you want to go home—

                    COBB
                   (sharp)
No, you don't.

                    ARTHUR
But this can't be done.

> COBB
>
> It can. You just have to go deep enough.

> ARTHUR
>
> You don't know that!—

> COBB
>
> I've done it before.

Arthur is taken aback. Cobb turns to the window.

> ARTHUR
>
> Did it work?

> COBB
> (quiet)
>
> Yes.

> ARTHUR
>
> Who did you do it to?

Cobb looks at Arthur. Closed. Arthur shrugs.

> ARTHUR
>
> So why are we headed to Paris?

> COBB
>
> We're going to need a new architect.

INT. GREAT HALL, ÉCOLE D'ARCHITECTURE—MORNING

Cobb, carrying a shopping bag, looks into a lecture hall: no students, just a RUMPLED PROFESSOR hunched over paperwork.

INT. LECTURE HALL—CONTINUOUS

> COBB (O.S.)
>
> You never did like your office.

PROFESSOR MILES looks up, squinting. Recognizes Cobb.

> MILES
>
> No space to think in that broom cupboard.

Cobb steps down past the empty wooden rows.

MILES

Is it safe for you to be here?

COBB

Extradition between France and the U.S. is a bureaucratic nightmare.

MILES

I think they'd find a way to make it work in your case.

Cobb hand Miles the shopping bag.

COBB

Can you take these back for the kids?

MILES

It'll take more than the occasional stuffed animal to convince those children they still have a father.

COBB

I know. I thought you could talk to Marie about bringing them on vacation. Somewhere I could meet—

MILES

Why would she listen to me?

COBB

You were married for twenty years.

MILES

She blames me as much as you.

COBB

Doesn't she understand that my kids need me?

MILES

Yes, she does. We all do. Go back and face the music, Dom. Explain what Mal did.

COBB

Be realistic, Stephen. They'd never understand— they'd lock me up and throw away the key. Or worse.

> MILES

You think what you're doing now is helping your case?

> COBB

Lawyers don't pay for themselves. This is what I have. This is what you taught me.

> MILES

I never taught you to be a thief.

> COBB

No, you taught me to navigate other people's minds. But after what happened with Mal there weren't a whole lot of legitimate ways for me to use that skill.

Miles looks at Cobb.

> MILES

Why did you come here, Dom?

Cobb shifts slightly.

> COBB

I found a way home. A job. For powerful people. If I pull it off, I can get back to my family. But I need help.

Miles realizes something.

> MILES

My God. You're here to corrupt one of my brightest and best.

> COBB

If you have someone good enough, you have to let them decide for themselves. You know what I'm offering—

> MILES

Money?

> COBB

No, not just money: the chance to build cathedrals, entire cities—things that have never existed, things that *couldn't* exist in the real world...

> **MILES**
> Everybody dreams, Cobb. Architects are supposed to make those dreams real.

> **COBB**
> That's not what you used to say. You told me that in the real world I'd be building attic conversions and gas stations. You said that if I mastered the dream-share I'd have a whole new way of creating and showing people my creations. You told me it would *free* me.

Miles looks at Cobb, sad.

> **MILES**
> And I'm *sorry*. I was wrong.

> **COBB**
> No, you weren't. Your vision was a vision of pure creativity. It's where we took it that was wrong.

> **MILES**
> And now you want me to let someone else follow you into fantasy.

> **COBB**
> They won't actually come on the job, they'll just design the levels and teach them to the dreamers.

> **MILES**
> Design them yourself.

> **COBB**
> Mal won't let me.

Miles looks at Cobb. Appalled.

> **MILES**
> Come back to reality, Dom. Please.

> COBB
>
> You want to know what's real, Stephen? Your grandchildren waiting for their dad to come back. This job—this *last* job—is how I get there.

Miles looks down, fiddles with his papers.

> COBB
>
> I wouldn't be standing here if there were any other way. I can get home. But I need an architect who's as good as I was.

Miles looks Cobb in the eye. Decides.

> MILES
>
> I've got someone better.

INT. CORRIDOR—LATER

Miles and Cobb stand by as STUDENTS file out of a lecture.

> MILES
>
> Ariadne...

A young woman carrying books turns. This is ARIADNE.

> MILES
>
> I'd like you meet Mr. Cobb.

She sizes him up with quick eyes. Offers her hand.

> ARIADNE
>
> Pleased to meet you.

> MILES
>
> If you have a few moments, Mr. Cobb has a job offer to discuss with you.

> ARIADNE
>
> A work placement?

> COBB
> (smiles)
>
> Not exactly.

EXT. ROOFTOP, ÉCOLE D'ARCHITECTURE—MOMENTS LATER

Ariadne leans against the parapet, overlooking Paris. She unwraps a
sandwich, watching Cobb pull out a pad of GRAPH PAPER and a PEN. He
offers them. She bites her sandwich.

> COBB
>
> A test.

> ARIADNE
> (mouth full)
> Aren't you going to tell me anything?

> COBB
>
> Before I describe the job, I have to know you
> could do it.

> ARIADNE
>
> Why?

> COBB
>
> It's not, strictly speaking, legal.

Ariadne raises her eyebrows.

> COBB
>
> You have two minutes to draw a maze that takes
> me one minute to solve.

Ariadne takes the pad and pen. Cobb looks at his watch.

> COBB
>
> Go.

She starts DRAWING LINES on the grid, constructing a maze.

> COBB
>
> Stop.

Ariadne hands the pad and pen to Cobb. He glances at the pad, then,
looking her in the eye, TRACES the solution. She is taken aback. Cobb
RIPS off the sheet, hands the pad back.

> COBB
>
> Again.

She traces straight lines, CONCENTRATING...

> ### COBB
> Stop.

She hands Cobb the pad, a touch pleased. Cobb solves the puzzle instantly, as before. Her smile falls.

> ### COBB
> You'll have to—

She GRABS the pad, frustrated... but this time she FLIPS it over and starts drawing on the BLANK CARDBOARD of the back. Cobb watches, surprised. He smiles as he sees that she's drawing CIRCLES, creating a maze based on concentric rings.

Ariadne hands back the pad, defiant. Cobb takes the pen, starts the maze. This time he gets stuck. Nods.

> ### COBB
> (working the maze)
> More like it.

EXT. NARROW STREET, PARIS—DAY

Arthur stops at a warehouse door. Consults a piece of paper.

INT. WORKSHOP—CONTINUOUS

A large, dusty warehouse. The SLIDING DOOR cracks open. Arthur enters. Looks around, approvingly.

INT. SAME—LATER

Arthur DRAGS LAWN CHAIRS into the middle of the room. He erects a table. Lays out several SILVER CASES, unpacking them, laying out lines of tubing, MECHANISMS...

EXT. PARISIAN CAFE—DAY

Cobb and Ariadne sit at an outdoor table.

> ### COBB
> They say we only use a fraction of the true
> potential of our brains... but they're talking

about when we're *awake*. While we dream, the
mind performs wonders.

ARIADNE

Such as?

COBB

How do you imagine a building? You con-
sciously create each aspect, puzzling over it in
stages... But sometimes, when your imagination
flies—

ARIADNE

I'm *discovering* it.

COBB

Exactly. Genuine inspiration.

Cobb leans forwards and draws on the paper table cloth.

COBB

In a dream your mind *continuously* does that...

Cobb has drawn a circle made of two arrows.

COBB

It creates and perceives a world *simultaneously*.
So well that you don't feel your brain doing the
creating. That's why we can short-circuit the
process...

ARIADNE

How?

COBB

By taking over the creating part.

Cobb draws a straight line between the two arrows.

COBB

This is where you come in. You build the world
of the dream. We take the subject into that
dream, and let him fill it with his subconscious.

> ARIADNE
> But are you trying to fool him that the dream is actually real life?

> COBB
> (nods)
> While we're in there, we don't want him to realize he's dreaming.

> ARIADNE
> How could I ever get enough detail to convince him that it's real?

> COBB
> *Our dreams feel real while we're in them.* It's only when we wake up we realize things were strange.

Ariadne gestures around them–

> ARIADNE
> But all the textures of real life—the stone, the fabric... cars... *people*... your mind can't create all this.

> COBB
> It does. Every time you dream. Let me ask you a question: You never remember the beginning of your dreams, do you? You just turn up in the middle of what's going on.

> ARIADNE
> I guess.

> COBB
> So... how did we end up at this restaurant?

> ARIADNE
> We came here from...

Ariadne trails off, confused.

> COBB
> How did we get here? Where are we?

Ariadne THINKS, unable to remember. A FAINT RUMBLE begins.

ARIADNE
Oh my God. We're *dreaming*.

Cobb nods. The RUMBLE is BUILDING.

COBB
Stay calm. We're actually asleep in the workshop. This is your first lesson in shared dreaming, remember?

Ariadne looks around, mind REELING. Cobb BRACES–

The restaurant VIOLENTLY FRAGMENTS, EXPLODING AND IMPLODING
PARTICLES OF FURNITURE, WALLS, PEOPLE FLYING AROUND– Ariadne
WONDERS at the MAYHEM WHIRLING around them– Cobb SHIELDS his
head against the debris. She sees him–

ARIADNE
(shouting over noise)
If it's just a dream, why are you covering your—

Ariadne is WIPED FROM HER SEAT BY A MASSIVE BLAST and we–

CUT TO:

INT. WORKSHOP—DAY

Ariadne JOLTS awake.

COBB (O.S.)
Because it's never *just* a dream.

Ariadne turns to Cobb's voice. They are both sitting in the lawn chairs.
Arthur watches over them.

COBB
And a face full of glass hurts like hell, doesn't
it? While we're in it, it's real.

ARTHUR
That's why the military developed dream sharing—a training program where soldiers could
strangle, stab and shoot each other, then wake
up.

> ARIADNE
>
> How did architects get involved?

> COBB
>
> Someone had to design the dreams.
> (to Arthur)
> Let's go another five minutes—

> ARIADNE
>
> We were only asleep for five minutes? We
> talked for an hour at least...

> COBB
>
> When you dream, your mind functions more
> quickly, so time seems to pass more slowly.

> ARTHUR
>
> Five minutes in the real world gives you an hour
> in the dream.

> COBB
>
> Let's see how much trouble you can cause in
> five minutes.

And we–

CUT TO:

EXT. SAME PARISIAN STREET—DAY

Ariadne walks down the crowded street with Cobb. Cobb looks around
at the street, the cafe, approving.

> COBB
>
> It's good. You've got the cafe, the layout... you
> forgot the book shop but pretty much every-
> thing else is here.

Ariadne looks at the passers-by.

> ARIADNE
>
> Who are the people?

> COBB
>
> They're projections of my subconscious.

ARIADNE

Yours?

COBB

Sure—*you* are the dreamer, *I* am the subject. My subconscious populates your world. That's one way we get at a subject's thoughts—his mind creates the people, so we can literally *talk* to his subconscious.

ARIADNE

How else do you do it?

COBB

Architecture. Build a bank vault or a jail, something secure, and the subject's mind will fill it with information he's trying to protect.

ARIADNE

Then you break in and steal it.

COBB

Exactly.

Ariadne wonders at the detail of the street.

ARIADNE

I love the concrete sense of things—
(stamps foot)
Real weight, you know? I thought a dream space would be all about the visual, but it's the *feel* of things. Question is, what happens as you start to mess with physics...

She CONCENTRATES on the street. The street starts to BEND IN HALF—the buildings on either side FOLDING IN until they form the INSIDE OF A CUBE OF CITY, GRAVITY FUNCTIONING INDEPENDENTLY ON EACH PLANE. Ariadne looks up (or down) at the people on the opposite city surface. Cobb watches her excitement.

ARIADNE

It's something, isn't it?

> COBB
> (quiet)

Yes. It is.

As they walk, Ariadne notices more and more of the projections STAR-ING at her.

> ARIADNE

Why are they looking at me?

> COBB

Because you're changing things. My subcon-scious *feels* that someone else is creating the world. The more you change things, the quicker the projections converge on you.

> ARIADNE

Converge?

> COBB

They feel the foreign nature of the dreamer, and attack—like white blood cells fighting an infec-tion.

> ARIADNE

They're going to attack us?

> COBB

Just you, actually.

They walk along the street to where it joins the next gravitational plane. They step up onto the different plane and walk down the street towards a river. As Ariadne approaches, steps emerge from the flag-stone, and she leads Cobb up onto a small jetty. As she concentrates, pillars emerge and a BRIDGE starts to telescope out from the jetty. They step onto it as it grows. Cobb is impressed.

> COBB

It's beautiful... but if you keep on changing things...

People crossing the bridge STARE at Ariadne. Several of them BUMP her shoulder as they pass.

> ARIADNE

Mind telling your subconscious to take it easy?

> COBB
>
> That's why it's called *sub*conscious. I don't con-
> trol it.

The bridge now spans the Seine. Cobb marvels at it.

> COBB
>
> Arched stone, iron pillars... it's...

Cobb pauses, thinking. Remembering.

INSERT CUT: *Mal, hair blowing, turns to Cobb, smiling, laughing. He smiles back. They are on the same bridge.*

> COBB
>
> I know this bridge. This place is real—
> (serious)
> You didn't imagine it, you *remembered* it...

> ARIADNE
>
> (nods)
> I cross it every day on my way to the college.

> COBB
>
> Never recreate places from your memory.
> Always imagine new places.

> ARIADNE
>
> You have to draw from what you know—

> COBB
>
> (tense)
> Use pieces—a streetlamp, phonebooths, a type
> of brick—not whole areas.

Several people around them ECHO Cobb's attitude...

> ARIADNE
>
> Why not?

> COBB
>
> Because building dreams out of your own
> memories is the surest way to lose your grip on
> what's real and what's a dream.

ARIADNE
Did that happen to you?

Cobb says nothing. He stands there, staring at Ariadne. PEOPLE around her stop and look at her, hostile.

COBB
Look, this isn't about *me*—

Cobb reaches for Ariadne's arm, turns her to him-

ARIADNE
Is that why you need me to build your dreams?

A passerby GRABS Ariadne's shoulder-

COBB
Leave her alone—

More of the crowd join in, PULLING at Ariadne, holding her arms open- Cobb PULLS people off- the crowd PUSHES him away- Cobb sees someone WALKING PURPOSEFULLY through the crowd towards the helpless Ariadne- it is Mal. She approaches with even strides- Ariadne stares at her, uneasy.

ARIADNE
Wake me up, Cobb.

As Mal walks, she pulls out a LARGE KNIFE-

COBB
Mal, no!

ARIADNE
Wake me up!

Ariadne SCREAMS as Mal LUNGES at her with the knife and we-

CUT TO:

INT. WORKSHOP—DAY

Ariadne WAKES, BREATHING HARD. Arthur moves to her-

ARTHUR
It's okay.

> ARIADNE
>
> Why couldn't I wake?

> ARTHUR
>
> The only way to wake from inside the dream is
> to die.

Cobb, in the lawn chair opposite, PULLS his tubes out.

> COBB
>
> She'll need a totem.

> ARIADNE
>
> What?

> ARTHUR
>
> Some kind of personal icon. A small object that
> you can always have with you, and that no one
> else knows.

Cobb gets to his feet. Ariadne stares at him, furious. He heads to the
bathroom.

> ARIADNE
>
> That's some subconscious you've got, Cobb.
> (calls after him)
> She's a real charmer!

> ARTHUR
>
> Sounds like you've met Mrs. Cobb.

> ARIADNE
>
> (surprised)
> She's his wife?

Arthur nods, pulling off Ariadne's tubes.

> ARTHUR
>
> So. A totem. You need something small,
> potentially heavy...

INT. BATHROOM, WORKSHOP—CONTINUOUS

Cobb takes out his PEWTER SPINNING TOP. SPINS it on the marble
counter...

INT. WORKSHOP—CONTINUOUS

Ariadne looks at Arthur, puzzled.

> ARIADNE
>
> Like a coin?

> ARTHUR
>
> Too common. You need something that has a
> weight or movement that only *you* know.

INT. BATHROOM, WORKSHOP—CONTINUOUS

Cobb STUDIES the spin of the top as it decays, becoming more and more ECCENTRIC...

INT. WORKSHOP—CONTINUOUS

> ARIADNE
>
> What's yours?

Arthur holds out a DIE.

> ARTHUR
>
> A loaded die.

Ariadne reaches for it– Arthur snatches it away–

> ARTHUR
>
> I can't let you handle it. That's the point. No one
> else can know the weight or balance of it.

> ARIADNE
>
> Why?

> ARTHUR
>
> So when you examine your totem...

INT. BATHROOM, WORKSHOP—CONTINUOUS

Cobb's spinning top WOBBLES OVER.

> ARTHUR (O.S.)
>
> You know, beyond a doubt, that you're not in
> someone else's dream.

Cobb GRABS it like a drowning man reaching for a lifeline.

INT. WORKSHOP—CONTINUOUS

Ariadne thinks this over.

                    ARIADNE
        That's not an issue for me.

                     ARTHUR
        Why not?

                    ARIADNE
        Arthur, maybe you can't see what's going on,
        maybe you don't want to. But Cobb's got prob-
        lems he's tried to bury down there. I'm not
        going to *open my mind* to someone like that.

Ariadne gets to her feet. Walks away.

                   COBB (O.S.)
        She'll be back.

Arthur turns. Cobb is standing in the bathroom doorway.

                     COBB
        I've never seen anyone pick it up so fast. And
        one reality won't be enough for her now. When
        she comes back, get her building mazes.

                     ARTHUR
        Where will you be?

                     COBB
        I've got to talk to Eames.

                     ARTHUR
        Eames? But he's in Mombasa. Cobol's backyard.

                     COBB
        Necessary risk.

                     ARTHUR
        There are plenty of other thieves.

                     COBB
        We don't just need a thief. We need a forger.

INT. GAMBLING DEN, MOMBASA—DAY

Crowded, bustling, smoke-filled. A westerner (40's), shabby suit, is squeezed in at a dice game. This is EAMES. He FIDDLES with his last two chips.

> **COBB (O.S.)**
> Rub them against each other all you like, they're not going to breed.

Eames looks up to see Cobb.

> **EAMES**
> You never know.

Eames tosses down his last chips. The dice are rolled...

> **COBB**
> Drink?

Eames loses.

> **EAMES**
> You're buying.

Cobb follows Eames. Eames mysteriously produces two stacks of chips and puts them down in front of the cashier. Cobb pulls one off the top, squints at the embossed name.

> **COBB**
> Your spelling hasn't improved.

Eames GRABS the chip. Hands it to the cashier.

> **EAMES**
> Piss off.

> **COBB**
> How's your handwriting?

Eames takes his money. Smiles at Cobb.

> **EAMES**
> Versatile.

EXT. STREET, MOMBASA—CONTINUOUS

Eames leads Cobb down the quiet street.

> EAMES
> Word is, you're not welcome in these parts.

> COBB
> Yeah?

> EAMES
> There's a price on your head from Cobol Engineering. Pretty big one, actually.

> COBB
> You wouldn't sell me out.

Eames looks at Cobb, offended.

> EAMES
> 'Course I would.

> COBB
> (smiles)
> Not when you hear what I'm selling.

EXT. BALCONY OF A COFFEE HOUSE—LATER

A ramshackle balcony overlooking a busy street. Eames pours.

> COBB
> Inception.

Eames's glass stops halfway to his mouth.

> COBB
> Don't bother telling me it's impossible.

> EAMES
> It's perfectly possible. Just bloody difficult.

> COBB
> That's what I keep saying to Arthur.

EAMES

Arthur? You're still working with that stick-in-the-mud?

COBB

He's a good point man.

EAMES

The best. But he has no imagination. If you're going to perform inception, you need imagination.

COBB

You've done it before?

EAMES

Yes and no. We tried it. Got the idea in place, but it didn't take.

COBB

You didn't plant it deep enough?

EAMES

It's not just about depth. You need the simplest version of the idea—the one that will grow naturally in the subject's mind. Subtle art.

COBB

That's why I'm here.

EAMES

What's the idea you need to plant?

COBB

We want the heir to a corporation to break up his father's empire.

EAMES

See, right there you've got various political motivations, anti-monopolistic sentiment and so forth. But all that stuff's at the mercy of the subject's prejudice—you have to go to the basic.

COBB

Which is?

> EAMES
> The relationship with the father.
> (downs drink)
> Do you have a chemist?

Cobb shakes his head.

> EAMES
> There's a man here. Yusuf. He formulates his
> own versions of the compounds.

> COBB
> Let's go see him.

> EAMES
> Once you've lost your tail.
> (Cobb reacts)
> Back by the bar, blue tie. Came in about two
> minutes after we did.

> COBB
> Cobol Engineering?

> EAMES
> They pretty much own Mombasa.

Cobb glances over the balcony.

> COBB
> Run interference. We'll meet downstairs in half
> an hour.

> EAMES
> Back here?

> COBB
> Last place they'd expect.

Eames downs his drink. Rises. Walks over to the Businessman.

> EAMES
> Freddy!

The Businessman looks up, awkward.

> EAMES
>
> Freddy Simmonds, it *is* you!

Cobb nonchalantly SLIPS over the balcony DROPPING HARD into the midst of the crowd on the street below.

> EAMES
> (looks harder)
> Oh. No, it isn't.

The Businessman looks past Eames but Cobb has vanished.

EXT. STREET, MOMBASA—CONTINUOUS

Cobb stands up, PUSHES into the crowd- faces PEER at him- he moves, trying to blend- TURNS- a SECOND BUSINESSMAN is there.

> COBB
> (disarming smile)
> Yes?

> SECOND BUSINESSMAN
> We need to—

Cobb HEAD BUTTS the Second Businessman, PUSHES past him-

The First Businessman races out of the bar, sees Cobb's wake, DIVES after him- Cobb RACES headlong through tight passageways, WEAVING through or KNOCKING into the locals...

He steps into a dark, crowded cafe, scanning the tables... the First Businessman enters, spots him. An AFRICAN MAN gets in Cobb's face, jabbering at him in Swahili- Cobb considers his options... the First Businessman DRAWS A GUN- Cobb bolts, steps up on a table and out an open window, SCRAMBLING into the alley outside...

Cobb LOOKS left, right... CUTS LEFT into a narrow, CROWDED alley- the alley NARROWS TO A DEAD END. Faces in the CROWD start to watch Cobb- PEOPLE start to SURROUND him- Cobb looks back the way he came- the two Businessmen are there, GUNS DRAWN-

Cobb sees a SMALL GAP between the buildings at the narrow end- he THROWS himself into it- gets STUCK HALFWAY...

The crowd bears down, GRABBING for him as Cobb struggles to SQUEEZE HIMSELF through the gap... Cobb's moving INCHES as his pursuers gain

YARDS... the Crowd is upon him— he BURSTS FREE, TUMBLING onto the next street, ROLLING out of sight.

Cobb Jumps to his feet— in a market square. TWO MORE BUSINESSMEN move towards him. Cobb BOLTS but a CAR SKIDS UP, BLOCKS HIS PATH— the door opens— SAITO IS IN THE BACK.

> SAITO
> Care for a lift, Mr. Cobb?

> COBB
> (jumping in)
> What brings you to Mombasa, Mr. Saito?

> SAITO
> I have to protect my investment.

EXT. COFFEE HOUSE—MOMENTS LATER

Eames stands on the pavement. The car pulls up. Cobb beckons from the rear window. Eames looks at Saito. Back to Cobb.

> EAMES
> This is your idea of losing a tail?

> COBB
> (shrugs)
> Different tail.

INT. WORKSHOP—DAY

Arthur sits at the table, working on a mechanism. A small COUGH prompts him to look up: Ariadne is there.

> ARTHUR
> He said you'd be back.

> ARIADNE
> I tried not to come.

> ARTHUR
> But there's nothing else quite like it.

> ARIADNE
> No paper, no pens... nothing between you and
> raw, direct creation.

Arthur picks up his mechanism.

> ARTHUR
> Shall we take a look at paradoxical architecture?

Ariadne nods, takes off her coat and we–

                                                        CUT TO:

INT. PENROSE STEPS—LATER

Arthur leads Ariadne down some busy steps in a large glass and steel ATRIUM in an office complex.

> ARTHUR
> You're going to have to master a few tricks if you're going to build three complete dream levels.

A SECRETARY DROPS some papers as they pass...

> ARIADNE
> What sort of tricks?

They take a tight turn and continue down the next flight.

> ARTHUR
> In a dream, you can cheat architecture into impossible shapes. That lets you create closed loops, like the Penrose Steps. The infinite staircase.

Ariadne FREEZES– THEY ARE IN THE EXACT SPOT THEY STARTED DESCENDING FROM, next to the Secretary gathering her papers.

Ariadne puzzles at the impossible construction of the stairs.

> ARTHUR
> See...

Arthur stops her gently– they are on the highest step, with a LARGE DROP to the next step. Arthur gestures at the drop.

ARTHUR

Paradox. A closed loop like this helps you dis-
guise the boundaries of the dream you've created.

ARIADNE

How big do the levels have to be?

ARTHUR

Anything from the floor of a building, to an
entire city. But it has to be complicated enough
for us to hide from the projections.

ARIADNE

A maze.

ARTHUR

And the better the maze—

ARIADNE

The longer we have before the projections catch
us.

Ariadne looks around. Sees people LOOKING at Arthur.

ARIADNE

My subconscious seems polite enough.

ARTHUR

You wait, they'll turn ugly. No one likes to feel
someone else messing around in their mind.

ARIADNE

Cobb can't build anymore, can he?

ARTHUR

I don't know if he can't, but he won't. He thinks
it's safer if he doesn't know the layouts.

ARIADNE

Why?

ARTHUR

He won't tell me. I think it's Mal. I think she's
getting stronger.

> ARIADNE

His ex-wife?

> ARTHUR

She's not his ex.

> ARIADNE

They're still together?

Arthur turns to Ariadne. Gentle.

> ARTHUR

No. No, she's dead, Ariadne. What you see in there is just his projection of her.

> ARIADNE

What was she like in real life?

> ARTHUR
> (quiet)

She was lovely.

CUT TO:

EXT. ROOFTOP, OLD TOWN, MOMBASA—DAY

Saito deposits a FILE in front of Cobb: PHOTOS, DOCUMENTS. As Cobb runs through them, he passes them to Eames.

> SAITO

Robert Fischer, 32. Heir to the Fischer Morrow energy conglomerate. He's spent his whole life being groomed as successor—breaking up his father's empire will take a radical shift in his thinking.

> COBB

What's your problem with Fischer?

> SAITO

That's not your concern.

> COBB

This isn't the usual corporate espionage, Mr. Saito. This is *inception*. The seed of the idea we plant will grow in this man's mind. It'll change him. It might even come to define him.

Saito looks at Cobb.

> SAITO
> My sources suggest you might not have always been so cautious.

> COBB
> Then you need new sources, Mr. Saito.

Saito considers Cobb. Shrugs.

> SAITO
> Fischer Morrow has the regulators in their pockets. We're the last company standing between them and total energy dominance and we can no longer compete. Soon they'll control the energy supply of half the world. They'll be able to blackmail governments, dictate policy. In effect, they become a new superpower. The world needs Robert Fischer to change his mind.

> EAMES
> That's where we come in. How's Robert Fischer's relationship to his father?

> SAITO
> Rumor is the relationship is complicated.

> COBB
> We'll need more than rumor, Mr. Saito.

Eames picks up a photo: a distinguished executive (68).

> EAMES
> Can you get me access to him? Browning. Fischer senior's right-hand man. Fischer junior's godfather.

> SAITO
> It should be possible. If you can get the right references.

> EAMES
>
> References are something of a specialty for me,
> Mr. Saito.

EXT. DECREPIT BUILDING, MOMBASA—LATER

Eames leads Cobb and Saito down uneven steps to a doorway.

INT. STAIRWELL—CONTINUOUS

Peeling paint, buzzing flies. They ascend to a dusty, wire-reinforced glass door which Eames pushes open–

INT. PHARMACY—CONTINUOUS

Row upon row of wooden shelves holding hundreds of dusty glass bottles of all shapes and colors. At the far end, a portly 40-year-old man rises from behind his desk, beckoning. This is YUSUF.

> YUSUF
>
> Come, come.

Eames shakes Yusuf's hand. Yusuf stops at Cobb.

> YUSUF
>
> Ah, yes. Mr. Cobb. I've heard so very much
> about you.
>> (indicates chairs)
>
> Please.

Yusuf chases a CAT off Saito's chair.

> YUSUF
>
> Bloody cats.

Yusuf moves to a shelf and runs his fingers over the glass bottles. None of them has a label.

> YUSUF
>
> You work using Somnacin, I think, Mr. Cobb?

> COBB
>
> You're well informed, Mr. Yusuf.

Yusuf places a bottle on the desk in front of Cobb.

COBB
(dubious)
Somnacin?

YUSUF
(proudly)
Yusuf's Somnacin.

Yusuf pulls the stopper, holds it towards Cobb's nose.

COBB
As good as the real thing?

Yusuf WHIPS the bottle away from Cobb, offended.

YUSUF
Better.

Yusuf holds the bottle to the light, marveling.

YUSUF
Binds the dreamers tight. Let's them dream as
one. Makes it real. Of course, if you'd prefer, you
could use Somnacin brand. *If* you could explain
to the international control council what you
wanted it for.

Yusuf puts the bottle back onto the shelf. Sits.

YUSUF
You are seeking a chemist?
(Cobb nods)
To formulate compounds for a job?

COBB
And to come into the field with us.

YUSUF
I rarely go into the field, Mr. Cobb.

COBB
We need you there to tailor compounds to our
particular requirements.

YUSUF
Which are?

                    COBB

Great depth.

                    YUSUF

A dream within a dream? Two levels?

                    COBB

Three.

                    YUSUF

Not possible. That many dreams within dreams
would be too unstable.

                    COBB

I've done it before. You just have to add a sedative.

                    YUSUF

A *powerful* sedative. How many team members?

                    COBB

Five.

                    SAITO

Six.
                (to Cobb)
The only way to know you've done the job is if I
go in with you.

                    COBB

There's no room for tourists on these jobs, Mr.
Saito.

                    SAITO

This time, it would seem there is.

Cobb looks at him, uneasy. Yusuf pulls out another bottle.

                    YUSUF

Of course. I use it every day.

Yusuf hands it to Cobb, who considers the white liquid inside.

                    COBB

For what?

Yusuf beckons them further into the pharmacy, to a METAL DOOR. He
STOPS– second thoughts.

> YUSUF
> Perhaps... you will not want to see.

Cobb motions to continue. Yusuf pulls out a large key.

INT. BACK ROOM, PHARMACY—CONTINUOUS

A dark room with ROWS of low COTS. Each with a sleeping occupant.
Tubes connect their wrists. An ELDERLY BALD MAN watches over
them.

> EAMES
> (counting)
> Eighteen, twenty—all connected, bloody hell.

> YUSUF
> They come every day. To share the dream.

Yusuf nods at the Elderly Bald Man, who moves to the nearest bed.
Reaches out to the OCCUPANT. Gives his face a FIRM SLAP. The sleeper
does not even stir.

> YUSUF
> See? Very stable.

> COBB
> How long do they dream?

> YUSUF
> Three, four hours. Every day.

> COBB
> How long in dream time?

> YUSUF
> With this compound... about forty hours. Each
> and every day.

Saito surveys the room, appalled.

> SAITO
> Why do they do it?

> **YUSUF**
> Tell him, Mr. Cobb.

> **COBB**
> After a while...
> (looks at Saito)
> It becomes the only way you *can* dream.

> **YUSUF**
> Do *you* still dream, Mr. Cobb?

Cobb STARES at the sleepers. Uneasy.

> **EAMES**
> They come here every day to sleep?

> **ELDERLY BALD MAN (O.S.)**
> No.

Cobb turns to the Elderly Bald Man, who looks fondly at his dreamers.

> **ELDERLY BALD MAN**
> They come to be *woken up*... the dream has
> become their reality...

The Elderly Bald Man pokes a crooked finger at Cobb's chest.

> **ELDERLY BALD MAN**
> And who are *you* to say otherwise?

Cobb STARES at the Elderly Bald Man. DISTURBED. Cobb turns to Yusuf. TOSSES him the bottle.

> **COBB**
> Let's see what you can do.

INT. SAME—MOMENTS LATER

Cobb is lying on an empty cot, asleep. Yusuf stands over him. As we move in on Cobb's SLEEPING FACE we hear the sound of a FREIGHT TRAIN, BUILDING, and we—

CUT TO:

EXT. WASTELAND—DAY

CLOSE ON Cobb's face as he lies, EYES CLOSED, cheek pressed to a METAL RAIL- THE SOUND OF THE TRAIN IS DEAFENING- Cobb is BREATHING, BREATHING, BREATHING, and we–

CUT TO:

INT. BACK ROOM, PHARMACY—DAY

Cobb's eyes open. Yusuf is watching him.

> **YUSUF**
> Sharp, no?

Cobb nods. Gets to his feet, looking around–

INT. BATHROOM, PHARMACY—CONTINUOUS

Cobb SPLASHES water on his face, breathing hard- *INSERT CUT: A CURTAIN BILLOWS. MAL TURNS TO US, HAIR BLOWING, SMILING.* Cobb fumbles in his pockets, pulls out his spinning top. He tries to set it spinning on the back edge of the sink, but it FALLS to the floor and rolls towards the door– Saito is there. WATCHING Cobb. He looks down at the spinning top.

> **SAITO**
> Everything alright, Mr. Cobb?

Cobb dries his face with a paper towel. Picks up his top.

> **COBB**
> Everything's fine.

INT. BACK ROOM, WORKSHOP—NIGHT

Close on a small BRASS CHESS PIECE. Ariadne tips it over. Frowning, she picks up a micro drill, peels back the felt on the bottom and widens a hole in one side of its base. Tests the TIPPING POINT again. A NOISE makes her look up.

INT. WORKSHOP—CONTINUOUS

Ariadne comes into the main space. Someone is there, unpacking one of the MECHANISMS. Cobb.

> **ARIADNE**
> You're back.

Cobb looks up with a start. Caught out.

> **ARIADNE**
> Are you going under on your own?

> **COBB**
> I just—I need to test some things. I didn't realize anyone was here.

> **ARIADNE**
> Just working on my totem.

Ariadne holds up the chess piece. Cobb reaches for it.

> **COBB**
> Let me see—

Ariadne SNAPS it out of his reach. Smiles. Cobb nods.

> **COBB**
> You're learning.

> **ARIADNE**
> It's an elegant solution to keeping track of reality. Your invention?

> **COBB**
> No. Mal's.

Cobb pulls out his spinning top. Looks at it.

> **COBB**
> This one was hers. She'd spin it in a dream and it would never topple. Just spin and spin...

> **ARIADNE**
> Arthur told me she died.

COBB

She did. How are the mazes coming?

Ariadne indicates three large ARCHITECTURAL MODELS.

ARIADNE

Good. Each level relates to the part of the subject's subconscious we're trying to access. I'm
making the bottom level a hospital, so that
Fischer will bring his father there—

COBB

Don't tell me. Remember, you only want the
dreamer to know the layout.

ARIADNE

Why's that so important?

COBB

In case one of us brings in part of *our* subconscious. You wouldn't want any projections
knowing the layout—

ARIADNE

In case *you* bring Mal in.

Cobb says nothing.

ARIADNE

You won't build yourself because if you know
the maze, then she knows it. And she'd sabotage
the operation. You can't keep her out, can you?

Cobb says nothing.

ARIADNE

Do the others know?

COBB

No.

ARIADNE

You have to warn them if it's getting worse—

> COBB
> (gentle)
> I didn't say it's getting worse. Look, Ariadne, I need them for this job. I need *you* for this job. Without your help, I'll never get back to my children. And that's all I can care about right now.

> ARIADNE
> Why can't you go home, Cobb?

Cobb looks at her, deciding what to say.

> COBB
> They think I killed her.

> ARIADNE
> How did she die?

Cobb thinks.

INSERT CUT: *Mal, wind* BLOWING *her hair, smiles at Cobb. Now we see Cobb—* SHAKING HIS HEAD, TEARS STREAMING, BEGGING—

> COBB
> Thank you.

> ARIADNE
> For what?

> COBB
> Not asking whether I did.

INT. WORKSHOP—DAY

Ariadne, Arthur, Yusuf, Eames and Saito sit around the room, looking at FILES. Cobb presides.

> COBB
> The mark is Robert Fischer, heir to the Australian energy conglomerate, Fischer Morrow.

Cobb opens a large presentation pad.

COBB (reads aloud)
"I WILL SPLIT UP MY FATHER'S EMPIRE."

Cobb turns to the team.

COBB

An idea Robert Fischer's conscious mind would never accept. We have to plant it deep in his subconscious.

ARTHUR

How deep?

COBB

Three levels down.

ARTHUR

A dream within a dream within a dream? Is that even possible?

COBB

Yes. It is.

COBB

Now, the subconscious motivates through emotion, not reason, so we have to translate the idea into an *emotional* concept.

ARTHUR

How do you translate a business strategy into an emotion?

COBB

That's what we have to figure out. Robert and his father have a tense relationship. Worse, even, than the gossip columns have suggested...

EAMES

Do you play on that? Suggest breaking up his father's company as a 'screw you' to the old man?

COBB

No. Positive emotion trumps negative emotion every time. We *yearn* for people to be reconciled, for catharsis. We need *positive* emotional logic.

Eames thinks. Paces. Looking back at the board.

> **EAMES**
> Try this... "MY FATHER ACCEPTS THAT I WANT
> TO CREATE FOR MYSELF, NOT FOLLOW IN HIS
> FOOTSTEPS."

> **COBB**
> That might work.

> **ARTHUR**
> Might? We'll have to do better than that.

> **EAMES**
> Thanks for the contribution, Arthur.

> **ARTHUR**
> Forgive me for wanting a little specificity,
> Eames.

> **COBB**
> Inception's not about specificity. When we get
> inside his head, we're going to have to work
> with what we find.

Arthur shrugs, frustrated. And we–

CUT TO:

EXT. NEW YORK STREETS—DAY

The team are in the middle of a DESERTED intersection. Ariadne is showing Yusuf aspects of the geography.

> **EAMES**
> We could split the idea into emotional triggers,
> and use one on each level.

> **COBB**
> How do you mean?

> **EAMES**
> On the top level, we open up his relationship
> with his father.... Say: "I WILL NOT FOLLOW IN MY
> FATHER'S FOOTSTEPS." Next level down we've
> accessed his ambition and self-esteem.

We feed him: "I WILL CREATE SOMETHING MYSELF."
Then, the bottom level, we bring out the emotional big guns...

                    COBB
"MY FATHER DOESN'T WANT ME TO BE HIM."

                    EAMES
That could do it.

                    ARTHUR
How do you produce these emotional triggers?

                    EAMES
I forge each emotional concept in the style
and manner of Peter Browning, a key figure in
Fischer's emotional life.

Two AFRICAN PEDESTRIANS wander into view.

                    ARTHUR
Are those yours?

Eames shakes his head. Cobb turns to Yusuf.

                    ARTHUR
Yusuf?

                    YUSUF
Yup. Sorry.

                    COBB
Suppress them. We don't bring our own projections into the dream—we let Fischer's subconscious supply the people.

                    EAMES
Saito, when do I get to see Browning?

                    SAITO
You fly out to Sydney on Tuesday. We've
arranged for you to spend several days...

INT. ANTEROOM, MAURICE FISCHER'S OFFICE—DAY

Eames sits in the crowded room. Boxes and files are piled high. Browning stands by a pair of double doors.

> SAITO (V.O.)
> *...as part of a consulting litigation team working for Browning.*

> BROWNING
> I'm not smelling settlement here—we take them down.

> LAWYER
> Mr. Browning, Maurice Fischer's policy is always one of avoiding litigation—

Browning turns to the lawyer. Calm, but POWERFUL.

> BROWNING
> Shall we relay your concerns directly to Maurice?

Browning opens the doors to Maurice Fischer's inner office. Eames leans in to watch as Browning beckons the Lawyer into-

INT. MAURICE FISCHER'S INNER OFFICE—CONTINUOUS

The office is a MAKESHIFT HOSPITAL ROOM: a BED where the desk should be. Browning addresses a figure at the window. ROBERT FISCHER, 30's, abstracted.

> BROWNING
> How is he?

Fischer turns to Browning. Motions silence, as he glances at his FATHER in the bed. Wheezing gently.

> BROWNING
> I don't want to bother him unnecessarily but I know he—

> FATHER
> Robert! I've told you to keep out the damn!—

MAURICE LASHES OUT, KNOCKING things from his bedside table. A NURSE calms Maurice as Fischer crouches to retrieve a FRAMED PHOTOGRAPH. He looks at the photo through the broken glass– a YOUNG BOY holds a PINWHEEL CLEARLY MADE BY A CHILD (each of the points is numbered in pen), his FATHER blows on it.

> **BROWNING**
> Must be a cherished memory of his—

> **FISCHER**
> *I* put it by his bed. He hasn't even noticed.

> **BROWNING**
> Robert, we have to talk about a power of attorney. I know this is hard for you, but it's important that we start to think about the future—

> **FISCHER**
> Not now, Uncle Peter.

Browning looks at Fischer, considering. Biding his time.

> **EAMES (V.O.)**
> *The vultures are circling. The sicker Maurice Fischer becomes, the stronger Peter Browning becomes...*

Eames WATCHES Browning, STUDYING his every move.

INT. BATHROOM—DAY

Eames gestures at a mirror, as if offering to shake hands...

> **EAMES (V.O.)**
> I've had time to learn Browning's physical presence and mannerisms...

In the mirror: BROWNING GESTURES BACK.

INT. WORKSHOP—CONTINUOUS

> **EAMES**
> Now, in the dream, I can impersonate Browning and suggest the concepts to Fischer's conscious mind...

                    EAMES
              (draws a diagram)
        Then we take Fischer down another level and
        his own subconscious feeds it right back to him.

                    ARTHUR
              (impressed)
        So he gives *himself* the idea.

                    EAMES
        Precisely. That's the only way to make it stick. It
        has to seem *self-generated*.

                    ARTHUR
        Eames, I'm impressed.

                    EAMES
        Your condescension, as always, is much appreci-
        ated, Arthur.

                                                    CUT TO:

INT. DESERTED HOTEL LOBBY—DAY

        The team sit on the steps of the large marble lobby, debating. Ariadne
        is showing Arthur the lobby.

                    EAMES
        He's not scheduled for surgery, no dental, noth-
        ing.

                    COBB
        I thought he had some knee thing?

                    EAMES
        Nothing they'd put him under for. Besides, we
        need a good ten hours.

                    SAITO
        Sydney to Los Angeles.

        They turn to Saito.

> SAITO

Twelve hours and forty-five minutes—one of the longest flights in the world. He makes it every two weeks...

EXT. AIRFIELD—DAY

Fischer steps out of a black town car and walks across the tarmac towards a GULFSTREAM JET, accompanied by two aides.

> COBB (V.O.)

Surely he flies private?

> SAITO (V.O.)

Not if there were unexpected maintenance with his plane.

Fischer is met at the steps by a DISTRAUGHT FLIGHT OFFICER.

INT. HOTEL LOBBY—DAY

Cobb chews this over. Arthur comes over.

> ARTHUR

It'd have to be a 747.

> COBB

Why?

> ARTHUR

On a 747 the pilots are up above, first class is in the nose so nobody walks through the cabin. We'd have to buy out the whole cabin, and the first class flight attendant—

> SAITO

We bought the airline.

Everyone turns to Saito.

> SAITO

It seemed... neater.

> COBB

Neater, huh?
>> (gets to his feet)

>   Well, now we have ten uninterrupted hours.
>   (to Ariadne)
>   Nice lobby, by the way.
>
> And we–

CUT TO:

INT. WORKSHOP—DAY

The group is back in the workshop, deep in discussion.

>   ARTHUR
>   My question is how we go down three layers
>   with enough stability. Three layers down a little
>   turbulence is gonna translate into an *earth-
>   quake.* The dreams are gonna collapse with the
>   slightest disturbance.

Yusuf clears his throat.

>   YUSUF
>   Sedation. For sleep stable enough to create
>   three layers of dreaming...

INT. MAKESHIFT LAB—DAY

Yusuf depresses a plunger. Arthur is SLEEPING in a chair.

>   YUSUF (V.O.)
>   *We will have to combine it with an* extremely
>   *powerful sedative....*

Eames SLAPS Arthur, HARD. Arthur does not stir.

INT. WORKSHOP—DAY

Arthur unconsciously rubs his cheek.

>   YUSUF
>   The compound we'll be using to share the
>   dream is an advanced Somnacin derivative. It
>   creates a very clear connection between dream-
>   ers, whilst actually accelerating brain function.

COBB

Buying us more time in each level.

YUSUF

Brain function in the dream will be about twenty times normal. And when you go into a dream within that dream the effect is compounded.

ARIADNE

How much time?

YUSUF

Three dreams... that's ten hours, times twenty, times twenty, times twenty...

EAMES

Math was never my strong suit.

COBB

It's basically a week one layer down, six months two layers down—

ARIADNE

And *ten years* in the third level. Who wants to spend ten years in a dream?

YUSUF

Depends on the dream.

EAMES

It's not going to take us long to crack Fischer open once we get going. We'll be out in a couple days, max.

ARTHUR

How do we get out once we've made the plant?
(to Cobb)
I hope you've got something a little more elegant in mind than shooting me in the head like last time.

Arthur tilts back in his chair. Yusuf turns to Cobb.

COBB

A kick.

                    ARIADNE
        What's a kick?

Eames slips his foot under Arthur's chair leg. TIPS it– Arthur's legs
SHOOT UP INSTINCTIVELY for balance–

                    EAMES
        That, Ariadne, would be a kick.

                    COBB
        That feeling of falling which snaps you awake.
        We use that to jolt ourselves awake once we're
        done.

                    ARTHUR
        But how are we going to feel that through the
        sedation?

                    YUSUF
        That's the clever part. I customize the sedative...

INT. MAKESHIFT LAB—DAY

Cobb, Eames and Yusuf watch Arthur, ASLEEP, in a chair.

                    YUSUF (O.S.)
        To leave inner ear function unimpaired...

Yusuf, with a wicked grin, slowly TIPS Arthur's chair backwards... as
he falls, Arthur's body JERKS, EYES OPENING just before he HITS the
floor.

INT. WORKSHOP—DAY

Arthur thinks, nodding slowly.

                    YUSUF
        That way, however deep the sleep, the sleeper
        will still feel falling...

INT. MAKESHIFT LAB—DAY

Yusuf gleefully LEANS a SLEEPING ARTHUR to one side...

                    YUSUF (V.O.)
        Or tipping...

Arthur goes down with a CRASH, JERKING AWAKE–

INT. WORKSHOP—DAY

Arthur thinks this through.

> ARTHUR
> Even that won't cut through *three* layers of deep
> sleep.

> COBB
> The trick is to devise a kick for each level, then
> *synchronize* them to get a snap that penetrates
> all three layers.

Arthur looks at Cobb, getting it.

> ARTHUR
> We can use the musical countdown to synchro-
> nize the different kicks.

INT. WORKSHOP—NIGHT

Ariadne comes into the darkened main space. Cobb is lying on one of
the chairs, asleep. Plugged into the mechanism. Ariadne stands over
him. Watching.

She opens the case, PULLS one of the tubes, sits, checking the dials as
she injects the needle cap into her arm, and we–

CUT TO:

INT. CAGE STYLE ELEVATOR—DAY

Ariadne ascends. She looks at the buttons. Spots the "B." The elevator
STOPS. She looks through the grill at–

INT. YOUNG GIRL'S BEDROOM—DAY

Ariadne pulls back the grill and walks across the room, considering the
dusty furnishings. At the window is a doll's house, front slightly ajar.
Ariadne opens it. Inside is a SAFE. She tries it. LOCKED. A NOISE STAR-
TLES her– she turns, looking through a doorway into another room...

INT. LIVING ROOM—CONTINUOUS

Ariadne looks into the room to see Cobb and Mal talking, arguing. A private moment. Mal brushes at Cobb's hair, trying to convince him. We hear snatches of conversation–

> MAL
>
> You remember when you asked me to marry you?

> COBB
>
> Of course...

> MAL
>
> You said you had a dream...

> COBB
>
> That we'd grow old together.

> MAL
>
> And we can. You know how to find me... you know what you have to do.

Cobb is shaking his head, gently. Mal looks into Cobb's eyes– gentle, loving... Mal SPOTS Ariadne spying on them. FREEZES, staring, hostile. Cobb turns, sees Ariadne, moves towards her, leaving Mal.

> COBB
>
> You shouldn't be in here.

Cobb guides her back into the elevator.

> ARIADNE
>
> I wanted to know what "tests" you need to do on your own every night.

INT. CAGE STYLE ELEVATOR—DAY

Cobb shuts the CAGE DOOR. Ariadne hits a button. The elevator RISES. Through the GRILL Ariadne can see a BEACH stretching off into the distance. The elevator stops. Mal sits on the sand. Beside her, the two children are crouched, away from us, building a SANDCASTLE.

> ARIADNE
>
> Why do you do this to yourself?

COBB

This is the only way I can still dream.

ARIADNE

Is it so important to dream?

Cobb stares at his family.

COBB

In my dreams... we're still together.

The kids, WITHOUT TURNING AROUND, jump up and RUN AWAY.

INT. CAGE STYLE ELEVATOR—CONTINUOUS

The elevator descends.

ARIADNE

But these aren't just dreams, are they? They're
memories. You said never to use memories.

COBB

And I shouldn't.

ARIADNE

You're keeping her alive.

COBB

No.

ARIADNE

You can't let her go.

COBB

No. These are moments I regret. Moments I
turned into dreams so I could change them.

Ariadne's fingers move across the buttons– stop at the "B."

ARIADNE

What've you got buried down there that you
regret?

Cobb pushes her hand away. Hits the third floor button.

                              COBB

          There's only one thing I need you to understand
          about me...

INT. KITCHEN, COBB AND MAL'S HOUSE—MOMENTS LATER

Ariadne follows Cobb into the kitchen. A THIN MAN is there, standing
by the table. He holds a FOLDED PIECE OF PAPER.

                           ARIADNE

          This is your house?

                              COBB

          Mine and Mal's.

                           ARIADNE

          Where is she?

                              COBB

          She'd already died.

The Thin Man offers Cobb the piece of paper. A CHILD'S SHOUT– Cobb
TURNS. Ariadne follows his gaze to the garden. A small blonde boy
faces away from them, crouched on his haunches to look at something
on the ground.

                              COBB

          It's James. My boy. He's found something.
          Maybe a worm.

A slightly older girl RUNS into view.

                              COBB

          And there's Philippa.

She crouches beside the boy. Their FACES ARE AWAY FROM US. They
point and discuss whatever is on the ground.

                              COBB

          I thought about calling out, so they'd turn and
          smile those incredible smiles... but I'm out of
          time—

The Thin Man thrusts the paper into Cobb's hand.

> THIN MAN
>
> Right now. Or never, Cobb.

Cobb nods, turns from the window-

> COBB
>
> Then I panic that I'll always wish I'd seen them turn, that I can't waste this chance...

Cobb TURNS BACK to call out- but the children RACE OFF...

> COBB
>
> But the moment's passed. And whatever I do, the dream's always the same... When I'm about to call... they run.

Cobb watches them run off, calling for grandma, FACES UNSEEN.

> COBB
>
> If I'm going to see their faces again—I've got to get back here in the real world...

Behind him, Ariadne SLAMS the grill shut. Cobb TURNS.

INT. CAGE STYLE ELEVATOR—CONTINUOUS

Ariadne hits the BASEMENT button. The elevator starts to DESCEND. Ariadne STARES, fascinated as glimpses of floors slip past: Mal's childhood bedroom, a thundering wall of freight train... The elevator STOPS. Through the grill Ariadne sees a HOTEL SUITE. She pulls open the grill, steps cautiously out into-

INT. ELEGANT HOTEL SUITE—CONTINUOUS (NOW NIGHT)

DISHEVELED bedclothes, UPENDED room service table, STRAWBER-RIES across the floor. A STRUGGLE. Ariadne steps forwards- SMASH- she looks down to see that she has kicked over a CHAMPAGNE FLUTE. Ariadne feels a draught. The CURTAIN BILLOWS.

> MAL (O.S.)
>
> What are you doing here?

Ariadne TURNS. Mal is there.

                    ARIADNE
My name is—

                    MAL
I know who you are. What are you doing here?

                    ARIADNE
I don't know. Trying to understand.

                    MAL
How could you understand? Do you know what
it is to be a lover? To be half of a whole?

                    ARIADNE
No.

Mal moves slowly towards Ariadne...

                    MAL
I'll tell you a riddle. You're waiting for a train.
A train that will take you far away. You know
where you hope this train will take you, but you
don't know for sure...

Mal glides around Ariadne, looking her over.

                    MAL
But... *it doesn't matter.* How can it not matter to
you where that train will take you?

                    COBB (O.S.)
Because you'll be together.

Cobb is standing in the elevator. Mal nods. Looks at him.

                    MAL
How could you bring her *here*, Dom?

                    ARIADNE
What is this place?

                    COBB
A hotel. We spent our anniversaries in this suite.

                    ARIADNE
What happened here?

Mal picks up the BROKEN STEM of a champagne flute...

INT. CAGE STYLE ELEVATOR—CONTINUOUS

Cobb PULLS Ariadne into the elevator- Mal THROWS herself towards Ariadne- Cobb SLAMS the GRILL- Mal SMASHES against it AGAIN and AGAIN like a WILD ANIMAL- Ariadne FLINCHES-

> MAL
>
> YOU PROMISED! YOU SAID WE'D BE TOGETHER!—

> COBB
>
> We can. We will. But I need you to stay here for now—

> MAL
>
> YOU SAID WE'D GROW OLD TOGETHER!—

Cobb pushes a button and the elevator starts to rise.

> COBB
>
> I'll come back. I need you to stay here on your own for now. Just while I do this job. Then we can be together—

> MAL
>
> WE'LL BE TOGETHER—YOU PROMISED!—

Mal THROWS herself against the grill, and we-

CUT TO:

INT. WORKSHOP—NIGHT

Ariadne watches Cobb sleeping. His eyes gradually flicker open. He sees her watching him.

> ARIADNE
>
> You think you can just build a prison of memories to lock her in? You think that's going to contain her?

The LIGHTS COME ON: Saito and Arthur stand in the doorway.

> SAITO
>
> Maurice Fischer just died in Sydney.

> COBB

When's the funeral?

> SAITO

Thursday. In Los Angeles.

> COBB

Robert'll accompany the body Tuesday at the outside. We have to move.

Cobb gets up. Ariadne comes over to him.

> ARIADNE
> (low)

I'm coming with you.

> COBB

No. I promised Miles.

> ARIADNE

The team needs someone in there who understands what you're struggling with. If you don't want it to be me then you need to show Arthur what I just saw.

Cobb looks at Ariadne. Turns to Saito.

> COBB

We need one more seat on the plane.

INT. DEPARTURE GATE, SYDNEY—DAY

Saito stands looking out the window at a 747. Cobb arrives beside him. They watch a COFFIN being loaded.

> COBB

If I get on this plane and you haven't taken care of things... when we land I go to jail for the rest of my life.

> SAITO

Complete the job en route, I make one phone call from the plane... you will have no trouble clearing immigration.

INT. FIRST CLASS CABIN, 747—CONTINUOUS

The luxurious cabin has only ten seats. Cobb finds his– sees Ariadne in the seat behind his. They do not acknowledge each other. Behind her is Arthur, looking out the window. Eames enters, STUFFS his bag into the overhead bin, BLOCKING the passenger behind: ROBERT FISCHER, standing there, patient, bag in hand, wearing black.

> ### EAMES
> Oh, sorry.

Eames SQUEEZES up against his seat to let Fischer BRUSH PAST. Fischer moves to his seat, directly in front of Cobb. Eames TOSSES Cobb a PASSPORT. Cobb flips it open: Fischer's. Pockets it. Yusuf and Saito enter, take their seats.

EXT. RUNWAY—MOMENTS LATER

The 747 HURTLES down the runway.

INT. FIRST CLASS CABIN, 747—MOMENTS LATER

Cobb looks down at his hand: a TINY VIAL taped to the center of his palm. He removes the cap. The seatbelt sign goes dark. Cobb unbuckles, stands.

> ### COBB
> Excuse me?

Fischer looks up.

> ### FISCHER
> Yes?

> ### COBB
> I think this is yours...

Cobb holds up the open passport, comparing the picture to Fischer. Fischer's hand goes to his pocket. Cobb hands Fischer the passport.

> ### FLIGHT ATTENDANT
> Would you gentlemen care for a drink?

> ### FISCHER
> Water.

>   COBB
>   Same.

Fischer gives Cobb a thin smile. Holds up his passport.

>   FISCHER
>   Well, thank you.

>   COBB
>   No problem. Look, I couldn't help noticing your
>   name. You're not related to *Maurice* Fischer?

Fischer takes a beat. But Cobb seems harmless.

>   FISCHER
>   Actually, he was my father.

>   COBB
>   I'm very sorry for your loss. He was an inspiring
>   figure.

The Flight Attendant brings their drinks– Cobb takes them.

>   COBB
>   Thanks.

As he turns to Fischer he LOWERS his right hand... a CLEAR LIQUID DROPS into Fischer's water as Cobb hands it to him.

>   COBB
>   To Maurice Fischer.
>   (they drink)
>   I'll leave you in peace.

Fischer grants him a smile.

EXT. 747—LATER

The great plane SOARS through a burning cloudscape.

INT. FIRST CLASS CABIN, 747—MOMENTS LATER

Cobb reaches into the overhead for a blanket– lets it fall onto Fischer's head– Fischer doesn't flinch. ASLEEP. Cobb SIGNALS the others. The First Flight Attendant unlocks a CUPBOARD in the galley, then leaves, closing the curtain. Arthur moves into the galley and pulls out a MECHANISM CASE.

Cobb and Arthur open the mechanism– uncoil the tubes– feed them around the window side of each of the seats. Arthur rolls up Fischer's cuff– PUSHES the needle cap into Fischer's wrist. Arthur pulls Fischer's cuff down and hides the tubes behind the armrest of Fischer's seat.

Arthur runs the next tube to Ariadne. Cobb puts the case on Yusuf's lap. Yusuf checks the TIMERS, tapping the syringes. The others recline their seats. Yusuf HITS A BUTTON– closes the case– places it at his feet. He settles back, and we–

CUT TO:

INT. SEDAN—DAY

Cobb DRIVES. Saito and Arthur are in the back. Rain BEATS down. Cobb pulls over–

EXT. NEW YORK STREETS—CONTINUOUS

Yusuf stands on the corner, silver briefcase in hand, collar turned up against the rain. He reaches for the door.

INT. SEDAN—CONTINUOUS

Yusuf clambers into the back, brushing rain from his face.

ARTHUR
(indicates rain)
Couldn't you have peed before you went under?

YUSUF

Sorry.

The front door OPENS and Eames climbs in, soaked.

EAMES
Bit too much free champagne before takeoff, Yusuf?

YUSUF

Ha bloody ha.

> COBB
>
> At least we know he'll be looking for a cab in this.

INT./EXT. SEDAN ON RAINY NEW YORK STREETS—CONTINUOUS

Cobb pulls out into the heavy traffic. He weaves around several cars before lining up behind a YELLOW CAB.

> COBB
>
> Brace yourselves.

Cobb hits the gas– REAR ENDS the cab with a CRUNCH. The CABDRIVER gets out, fuming. Heads to Cobb's window–

> CABDRIVER
>
> Hey, asshole! Why don't you try driving without your thumb up—

He sees the SILENCED PISTOL Cobb is holding at his belly.

> COBB
>
> Walk away.

The Cabdriver backs off. Arthur climbs into the cab. Both cars pull away.

INT./EXT. CAB ON RAINY NEW YORK STREETS—CONTINUOUS

Arthur SLOWS in front of the TRAIN STATION, peering at the pedestrians. He SPOTS Fischer, lights the cab's sign. Fischer FLAGS him down. Fischer JUMPS into the back, brushing rain from his shoulders.

> FISCHER
>
> Third and Market. Snappy.

Eames JUMPS in from the other side.

> FISCHER
>
> What're you doing?

> EAMES
>
> Sorry, I thought it was free. Maybe we could share.

EAMES: SORRY, I THOUGHT IT WAS FREE. MAYBE WE COULD SHARE.

AMBUSH/TRAIN 4/24/09

1 CAB ON RAINY STREET.

2 EAMES + FISCHER IN THE BACK SEAT.

FISCHER "PULL OVER SO THIS GUY CAN..."

3 SAITO TURNS — POINTS A GUN AT FISCHER.

4

FISCHER HANDS
OVER HIS WALLE

CUT

5A

EAMES SMILES

"I'M AFRAID,

SHOT
CONT'D

5B

A SHOT SHATTE
THE WINDOW
BEHIND HIM.

CUT

7

ARTHUR REACTS —
HITS THE GAS.

(CUT)

8

THE CAB SPEEDS
FORWARD.·

(CUT)

9A

OVER ARTHUR
AS..

SHOT
CONT'D

9B

AN SUV
SLIDES IN
SIDEWAYS.

10

ARTHUR REACTS

11

THE SUV
BLOCKS TH[E]
CA[D].

3A

LONG LENS ON
FRONT OF TRAIN
AS IT CLIPS
THE FRONT OF
COBB'S CAR...

SHOT
CONT'D

TRAIN

18 B

CMT

19

THE TRAIN CREATES A WALL BETWEEN

ARTHUR TURNS to BACK UP. A 2ND SUV PULLS UP — BLOCKING THE CAB FROM BEHIND.

21

SECURITY MEN
ADVANCE THROUGH
TRAFFIC.

CUT

22

THEY FIRE INTO
THE CAB.

CAM
W/SECURITY

CUT

23

EAMES THROWS
HIMSELF ON
TOP OF FISCHER

CUT

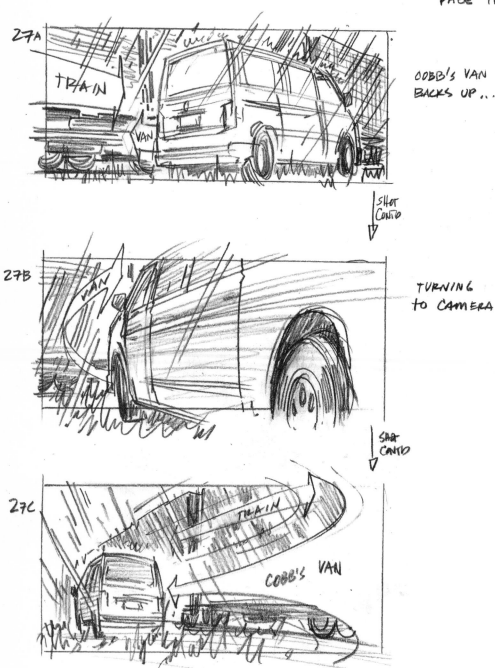

27A

TRAIN

VAN

COBB'S VAN
BACKS UP...

SHOT
CONT'D

27B

VAN

TURNING
to CAMERA

SHOT
CONT'D

27C

TRAIN

COBB'S VAN

                    FISCHER
    Maybe not.

Saito gets into the front passenger seat. Pointing a gun.

                    FISCHER
    Great.

Arthur pulls away. Fischer pulls out his wallet and tosses it at Eames.

                    FISCHER
                (contemptuous)
    There's 500 dollars in there. And the wallet's
    worth more than that. For that you ought to at
    least drop me at my stop.

Eames smiles at this.

                    EAMES
    I'm afraid—

A SHOT SHATTERS the window by Eames's head– another SHOT IMPACTS
by Saito–

                    EAMES
    Get us out of here!

Arthur hits the gas, but a BLACK S.U.V. SKIDS sideways in front, BLOCK-
ING the path–

A BLOCK BEHIND– Cobb is at a light. ARIADNE is getting in the front.
Cobb has HEARD the GUNFIRE–

                    COBB
    Come on!—

Cobb looks ahead to the AMBUSH, hits the gas– the sedan ROCKETS
forwards... but BAM– A FREIGHT TRAIN CLIPS THE FRONT OF THE SEDAN,
SHOVING IT SIDEWAYS AS AN ENDLESS TRAIN BARRELS PAST, A WALL
BETWEEN COBB AND THE AMBUSH–

A SECOND S.U.V. is behind the cab– PLAIN CLOTHES SECURITY MEN
advance through the traffic, weapons trained on the cab. Bullets RIP
into the cab as Eames throws himself on top of Fischer, PULLING a
SACK over his head–

Inside the sedan, Ariadne watches the train passing–

> **ARIADNE**
> This wasn't in the design—

Cobb BACKS UP, SPINS around, heading for the tail of the train–

A Security Man emerges from the front S.U.V. carrying an AUTOMATIC RIFLE– he steps towards the cab through the rain, raises his weapon and BLASTS THE CAB'S WINDSCREEN–

Cobb clears the end of the train, and SKIDS across the tracks–

Arthur CROUCHES down– PUSHES the accelerator with his HAND– YANKS the wheel– FLYING BLIND. The cab NAILS the Security Man, CRUNCHING into the front S.U.V.–

Cobb SMASHES his car into the rear S.U.V., creating a GAP–

Arthur YANKS the transmission and REVERSES– SCRAPING through the gap– Security Men DIVE out of the way– Arthur throws a ragged J-turn to head down a SIDE STREET– Cobb follows in the other car. Rain whips across Arthur's face as he BREATHES–

> **ARTHUR**
> Everybody okay? Saito?

Arthur looks at Saito. Saito's hand is at his belly. Covered in BLOOD.

EXT. WAREHOUSE—MOMENTS LATER

The sedan and cab pull into the side entrance– Eames jumps out– PULLS the shutter down behind them–

INT. WAREHOUSE—CONTINUOUS

Yusuf and Eames PULL Fischer from the cab, HUSTLING him through a doorway. Cobb JUMPS out of the sedan, furious.

> **COBB**
> Arthur! Arthur what the—

Arthur pulls the bloody Saito from the front seat.

> **COBB**
> Oh, Christ. Is he dying?

ARTHUR

I don't know. What happened back there?
Where were you?

COBB

We were blocked by a freight train.

ARTHUR
(to Ariadne)
Why would you put a train crossing in a downtown intersection?

ARIADNE

I didn't.

COBB
(snaps)
Why were we all ambushed, Arthur?! Those
weren't regular projections—they'd been
trained!

ARIADNE

How could they be trained?

ARTHUR

Fischer's had an extractor teach his mind to
defend itself. His subconscious is militarized. It
should've shown on the research—

COBB

So why the hell didn't it?!

ARTHUR

Calm down.

COBB

Don't tell me to calm down—you were meant
to check Fischer's background thoroughly. You
can't make this kind of mistake—we're not pre-
pared for this kind of violence—

ARTHUR

Cobb, we've dealt with sub-security before. We
just have to be more—

COBB

This wasn't part of the plan, Arthur!
(points at Saito)
He's *dying*!

EAMES (O.S.)

So we put him out of his misery.

Eames steps into the room, pulls his gun and moves over Saito.

COBB

No.

EAMES

He's in agony. Let's wake him up—

Cobb GRABS Eames's arm.

COBB

No!
(they lock eyes)
It won't wake him up.

EAMES

What do you mean, it won't wake him? When
you die in a dream you wake up.

YUSUF

Not from this. We're too heavily sedated to
wake up that way.

Eames looks at Yusuf, then to Cobb.

EAMES

So what happens if one of us dies?

COBB

That person doesn't wake up. Their mind drops
into Limbo.

ARIADNE

Limbo?

ARTHUR

Unconstructed dream space.

> ARIADNE
>
> What's down there?

> ARTHUR
>
> Raw, infinite subconscious. Nothing there but what was left behind by anyone on the team who's been trapped there before. On this team... just Cobb.

> ARIADNE
>
> How long would we be stuck there?

> YUSUF
>
> You couldn't even think about trying to escape until the sedation eases—

> EAMES
>
> How long?

> YUSUF
>
> Decades—it could be infinite—I don't know! Ask him—he's the one who's been there before!

Eames moves to Cobb. Looks him in the eye.

> EAMES
>
> Great. So now we're stuck in Fischer's mind battling it out with his private army, and if we get hit we're stuck in Limbo 'til our brains dissolve into scrambled egg?

Cobb says nothing. Saito groans more loudly.

> ARTHUR
>
> Let's just get him upstairs.

INT. OFFICÉ, WAREHOUSE—MOMENTS LATER

Saito is laid out on an old desk. Arthur examines him. He motions to Ariadne. Eames watches Cobb.

> ARTHUR
>
> Hold this. Firm pressure.

Arthur turns to Cobb.

ARTHUR

You knew the risks and you didn't tell us.

COBB

There wasn't meant to be any risk. We weren't
supposed to be dealing with a load of gunfire.

ARTHUR

You had no right.

COBB

It's the only way you can go three layers deep,
Arthur.

Arthur turns to Yusuf, hostile.

ARTHUR

And you. You went along with this?

YUSUF

I trusted him.

ARTHUR

You trusted him? When? When he promised
you half his share?

YUSUF
(offended)
No! His whole share. Plus, he told me he'd done
it before.

Arthur turns to Cobb.

ARTHUR

Oh, yeah? With Mal? That worked out great,
didn't it, Cobb?

Cobb grabs Arthur.

COBB

You don't know anything about that. This was
the only way to do this job, Arthur. I did what I
had to do to get back to my children.

EAMES

So you led us into a war zone with no way out.

COBB

We have a way out. The kick. We just have to
push on, do the job as fast as possible and get
out using the kick.

EAMES

Forget it. We go any deeper, we just raise the
stakes. I'm sitting it out on this level.

COBB

You'll never make it, Eames. Fischer's security
is surrounding this place as we speak. The
ten hours of the flight is a week at this level—
you'll never make it without getting killed.
Downwards is the only way forwards. We have
to carry on.

Saito groans. Cobb looks at him—

COBB

And we have to do it fast.

Eames and Arthur weigh this.

COBB

Eames, go get ready. Arthur, let's get in there
and soften him up.

INT. BATHROOM, WAREHOUSE—LATER

Cobb and Arthur, wearing BALACLAVAS, PULL the sack from Fischer's
head. He is chained to the radiator.

FISCHER

I'm insured against kidnapping up to ten million—this'll be simple—

COBB

No, it won't.

Fischer looks at Cobb, unnerved.

ARTHUR

In your father's office, below the bookshelves, is
his personal safe. We need the combination.

FISCHER

I never noticed a safe—

COBB

Doesn't mean you don't know the combination.

FISCHER

Well, I don't.

ARTHUR

We have it on good authority that you do.

FISCHER

Whose?

INT. OFFICE, WAREHOUSE—CONTINUOUS

Yusuf looks through Fischer's wallet. Eames is opening a HINGED, THREE-WING MIRROR.

YUSUF

Five hundred dollars, this cost?

EAMES

What's inside?

YUSUF

Cash, cards, ID... and this—

Yusuf holds up a SNAPSHOT: the photo from Maurice Fischer's office—YOUNG ROBERT holds his HOMEMADE PINWHEEL, his FATHER blows on it. Eames takes it from Yusuf. STUDIES it. Cobb enters. Eames hands him the snapshot.

EAMES

Useful?

Cobb studies the snapshot. Eames examines himself in the hinged mirror from multiple angles: ONE BY ONE the myriad Eames reflections BECOME BROWNINGS. Cobb pockets the photo.

COBB

You're on. You've got an hour.

> EAMES

An hour? I was supposed to have all night to
crack him.

> COBB

And Saito was supposed to keep his guts on the
inside. You've got an hour—get something we
can use.

Eames turns from the mirror AS BROWNING. He glances at his watch,
then SCREAMS, as if begging for mercy–

INT. BATHROOM, WAREHOUSE—CONTINUOUS

Browning's CRY reverberates– Fischer looks up, concerned–

> FISCHER

What's that?

> ARTHUR

Good authority.

Another cry rings out. Fischer recognizes the voice.

> FISCHER
Uncle Peter?! Make them stop—

> ARTHUR

The combination.

> FISCHER

I don't know it!

> ARTHUR
Why would Browning tell us you did?

> FISCHER
Let me talk to him—I'll find out.

INT. BATHROOM, WAREHOUSE—MOMENTS LATER

Cobb pushes Browning (Eames), bloody and bruised, into the room
and forces him down next to Fischer. Cobb handcuffs Browning's wrist
to a metal bracket on the side of the sink.

COBB

You've got an hour. Get talking.

Cobb leaves.

BROWNING (EAMES)

They've had me for two days. They've got someone with access to your father's office and they're trying to open his safe—they thought I'd know the combination, but I don't—

FISCHER

Neither do I, Uncle Peter.

BROWNING
(confused)

Maurice told me that after he passed only you would be able to open it.

FISCHER

He never gave me the combination.

Browning thinks for a minute. Realizes something.

BROWNING

He did, he just didn't tell you that it was a combination.

FISCHER

What, then?

BROWNING

Something only you would know. Some meaningful combination of numbers from your experiences with Maurice—

FISCHER

We didn't *have* a lot of meaningful experiences together.

BROWNING

Perhaps after your mother died...

                    FISCHER
After my mother died, I went to him in my grief.
You know what he told me? "There's really noth-
ing to be said, Robert."

                    BROWNING
He always had a hard time with emotional—

                    FISCHER
I was *eleven*, Uncle Peter.

Browning (Eames) takes this in.

                    BROWNING
He loved you, Robert. In his way.

                    FISCHER
"In his way?" At the end he called me to his
deathbed. He could barely speak, but he took
the trouble to say one last thing to me. He
pulled me close... I could make out only one
word. "Disappointed."

Browning can say nothing.

INT. OFFICE, WAREHOUSE—CONTINUOUS

Cobb pulls off his balaclava. Looks down at Saito, who is breathing
fast, shallow.

                    COBB
        How's he doing?

                    ARIADNE
        He's in a lot of pain.

Cobb takes Saito's hand. Looks him in the eye.

                    COBB
        When we get you down to the next level, the
        pain will be less intense.

Saito nods, breathing hard.

> ARIADNE
> (low)
> And if he dies?

> COBB
> His conscious mind will drop out of the dream.
> He'll be trapped in Limbo for a *lifetime*...

> ARIADNE
> What will that do to him?

Cobb looks at her. Grave.

> COBB
> When he wakes... his mind could be completely
> gone.

> SAITO
> When... when we wake I will still honor our
> arrangement...

Cobb looks down at Saito sadly.

> COBB
> Saito-san, when you wake you might not even
> remember that we *had* an arrangement. You'll
> have forgotten this world. Limbo will be your
> reality. Lost there so long, you'll have become
> an old man...

> SAITO
> Filled with regret?

> COBB
> Waiting to die alone. Yes.

> SAITO
> Then I'll take the chance and come back. And
> we'll be young men together again.

Saito smiles weakly. Cobb nods at him, turns to Ariadne.

> ARIADNE
> When were you trapped in Limbo?

Cobb says nothing. Ariadne pulls him away from Saito.

> ARIADNE
>
> Cobb, you might have convinced the rest of this team to carry on with the job. But they don't know the truth.

> COBB
>
> What truth?

> ARIADNE
>
> The truth that at any minute you might bring a *freight train* through the wall. The truth that Mal is bursting up through your subconscious. The truth that as we go deeper into Fischer, we're also going deeper into you—and I'm not sure we're going to like what we find there.

Cobb stares back at Ariadne. Saying nothing.

> ARIADNE
>
> This is not just about Fischer, it's about you. Tell me what happened to you and Mal. Trapped in Limbo.

Cobb looks at her. Thinking it through.

> COBB
>
> We were on a job. Exploring dreams within dreams. But we didn't understand how your mind can turn hours into years. How you can get trapped. Trapped so deep that when you wash up on the shore of your subconscious...

INSERT CUT: MAL LIES ON THE SAND, STARING UP AT A CLOUDLESS SKY, WAVES WASHING OVER HER...

> COBB
>
> You can lose track of what's real.

> ARIADNE
>
> How long were you stuck?

Cobb pauses before he answers. Looks at Ariadne.

> COBB
>
> Fifty years.

Ariadne stares at him, incredulous.

> **ARIADNE**
> How did you stand it?

INSERT CUT: COBB AND MAL BUILD A SANDCASTLE ON THE BEACH...

> **COBB**
> We built. We created a whole world for our-
> selves...

INSERT CUT: COBB AND MAL WALK THROUGH A DESERTED CITY.

> **COBB**
> It's not so bad at first, being gods. The problem
> is knowing that it's not real. It became impos-
> sible for me to live like that.

> **ARIADNE**
> But not for her?

> **COBB**
> She accepted it. At some point...

INSERT CUT:

INT. MAL'S CHILDHOOD HOME—DAY

*Mal opens a DOLL'S HOUSE. Inside is a SAFE. She opens it– it is empty.
She pulls out her SPINNING TOP.*

> **COBB (V.O.)**
> *...she'd decided to forget that our world wasn't
> real.*

Mal places the top inside the safe. LOCKS IT AWAY...

INT. OFFICE, WAREHOUSE—CONTINUOUS

> **ARIADNE**
> And when you finally woke up?

> **COBB**
> To wake from that. From decades lived. To be
> old souls thrown back into youth. It was hard.
> At first Mal seemed okay. But I started to real-

ize something was wrong. Finally she admitted it. This idea she was possessed by. This simple little idea that changed everything...

> ARIADNE
>
> What was it?

> COBB
>
> That our world was not real. No matter what I did, no matter what I said, she was convinced that we were still in a dream. That we needed to wake up again...

INT. COBB AND MAL'S KITCHEN—DAY (FLASHBACK)

Cobb is trying to calm Mal, who is hysterical.

> COBB (V.O.)
>
> *That to get home we'd have to kill ourselves.*

INT. WORKSHOP—DAY

Ariadne looks at Cobb, appalled.

> ARIADNE
>
> What about your children?

Cobb has to look away.

> COBB
>
> She... she believed they weren't real. That our *real* children were waiting. Somewhere above...

INT. COBB AND MAL'S KITCHEN—DAY (FLASHBACK)

Mal shakes her head at Cobb as he USHERS the children out of the room, FACES UNSEEN—

> COBB
>
> Calm down, Mal—

> MAL
>
> They're projections, Dom. Your dreams. I'm their mother—don't you think I can tell the difference?

Cobb closes the door– turns to her, eyes full of bitter tears.

> **COBB**
> If it's my dream then why can't I control it? Why can't I stop this?

> **MAL**
> (it's obvious)
> You don't know you're dreaming.

> **COBB**
> You keep telling me I am—

> **MAL**
> And you don't believe me!

> **COBB (V.O.)**
> *She was certain. But she loved me too much to go without me. So she made a plan...*

INT. ELEGANT HOTEL CORRIDOR—NIGHT (FLASHBACK)

Cobb walks along, checking door numbers against a key.

> **COBB (V.O.)**
> *For our anniversary...*

INT. ELEGANT HOTEL SUITE—CONTINUOUS (FLASHBACK)

Cobb enters the lavish suite. He notices the DISHEVELED BEDCLOTHES. He steps forwards– SMASH– he has tipped over a champagne glass with his foot... dinner for two is SPREAD ACROSS THE FLOOR. He looks at the DEBRIS, confused... next to the broken glass is a SPINNING TOP. He picks it up, studying it, thinking. He feels a draught, looks to the window. The CURTAIN BILLOWS.

EXT. EXTERIOR ATRIUM—CONTINUOUS (FLASHBACK)

Cobb looks out the window: Mal sits on the ledge of the opposite window. HAIR BLOWING. Feet dangling over the dizzyingly high atrium. She smiles.

> **MAL**
> Join me.

                    COBB

Mal, come back inside.

                    MAL

No. I'm going to jump. And you're coming with
me.

                    COBB

No, I'm not. This is *real*—if you jump, you're not
going to wake up, you're going to *die*. Let's go
back inside and talk about this, please.

                    MAL

We've talked enough.

She KICKS off a shoe and watches it DROP.

                    MAL

Come out onto the ledge or I'll jump right now.

She means it. Cobb swings his legs out, sitting on the ledge opposite
his wife. He looks down at the drop.

                    MAL

I'm asking you to take a leap of faith.

                    COBB

I can't do that, Mal. I can't leave our children.

                    MAL

If I go without you, they'll take them away, any-
way.

                    COBB

What do you mean?

                    MAL

I filed a letter with our attorney. Explaining how
I'm fearful for my safety, how you've threatened
to kill me...

Cobb looks back at the wrecked hotel suite, PANICKING...

> MAL

I love you, Dom. I've freed you from the guilt of choosing to leave them. We're going home to our real children.

> COBB

Our children are here, Mal.

Mal CLOSES HER EYES. Cobb looks for some way to reach her...

> MAL

You're waiting for a train...

> COBB

NO! MAL, NO, I CAN'T!

> MAL

A train that will take you far away...

> COBB

DON'T DO THIS!

> MAL

You know where you hope this train will take you, you can't know for sure...

> COBB

DON'T!

> MAL

But it doesn't matter...

> COBB

NO!

> MAL

Because you'll be together—

Mal SLIPS FORWARDS INTO SPACE. Cobb SCREAMS after her. Then tries to bury his face in the wall...

INT. OFFICE, WAREHOUSE—DAY

Cobb stares as he remembers.

> COBB
>
> Her letter to the authorities refuted all the
> claims about her sanity that she knew I'd make...

INT. COBB AND MAL'S KITCHEN—DAY (FLASHBACK)

Cobb stands with the Thin Man, who has a piece of paper.

> COBB (V.O.)
>
> *She'd had herself declared sane by three differ-*
> *ent psychiatrists.*

Cobb hears a SHOUT– turns to the garden. James CROUCHES, Philippa
joins him, examining the ground, FACES UNSEEN...

> COBB (V.O.)
>
> *It was impossible for me to explain the nature of*
> *her madness...*

The Thin Man thrusts the paper into Cobb's hand.

> THIN MAN
>
> Right now. Or never, Cobb.

Cobb turns back to the window– about to call out– James and Philippa
RUN OFF. Cobb turns from the window. Looks at the paper in his hand.
It is an AIRPLANE TICKET.

> COBB (V.O.)
>
> *So I ran. And I've been running ever since, trying*
> *to buy my way back to my family...*

INT. OFFICE, WAREHOUSE—DAY

Cobb looks across at Ariadne.

> ARIADNE
>
> Psychiatrists judged her sane?

> COBB
>
> She *was* sane. She was just lost in the labyrinth.

> ARIADNE
>
> Then why should you blame yourself?

> COBB

Because we were a family. And we had a life I would do anything to get back to now. But that reality wasn't enough for me then.

> ARIADNE

It might have been your idea to push the limits, Cobb. But you're not responsible for the idea that destroyed her. The idea that her world wasn't real... that was her own idea from her own mind.

Cobb says nothing.

> ARIADNE

Your guilt defines her. Powers her. If we're going to succeed in this, you're going to have to forgive yourself, and you're going to have to confront her. But you don't have to do it alone.

> COBB

You don't have to do this for me—

> ARIADNE

I'm doing it for the others. They don't know the risk they've taken coming in here with you.

Cobb looks at the rooftop opposite, sees a SNIPER take up a position. Cobb shakes his head, frustrated.

> COBB

We can't stay here. Arthur?!

INT. BATHROOM, WAREHOUSE—CONTINUOUS

Browning puts his hand on Fischer's shoulder.

> BROWNING

These people are going to kill us if we don't give them the combination.

> FISCHER

They won't, they'll try to ransom us—

BROWNING

I heard them—they're going to lock us in and run the van into the river.

FISCHER

What *is* in the safe?

BROWNING

Something for you. Maurice always said it was his most precious gift... a *will*.

FISCHER

Maurice's will is with Port and Dunn.

BROWNING

It's an alternate. It supersedes the other only if *you* want it to.

FISCHER

What does it say?

BROWNING

It splits all the component businesses of Fischer Morrow into individual companies, transferring ownership to the boards of those companies...

FISCHER

Leaving me nothing?

BROWNING

A basic living. Nothing more. The entire empire would cease to exist.

FISCHER

Destroy my own inheritance? Why would he suggest such a thing?

BROWNING

I don't know, Robert.

Cobb OPENS the door. Arthur is behind him.

COBB

Come to your senses?

> FISCHER
>
> Let us go. I don't know the combination. Not
> consciously.

Cobb considers this. Opens his phone. Pulls out his gun.

> COBB
>
> Let's try instinctively. I have someone standing
> in your father's office ready to tap in a combina-
> tion.

He holds the phone to Fischer's mouth.

> COBB
>
> First six numbers that come into your head.
> Right now.

> FISCHER
>
> I have no idea—

Cobb SWINGS the gun onto Browning...

> COBB
>
> RIGHT NOW!

> FISCHER
>
> Five, two, eight... four, nine, one.

Cobb lowers his weapon. Listens to the phone. Shakes his head. Shuts
the phone.

> COBB
>
> You'll have to do better. Bag 'em.

Arthur puts SACKS over their heads.

INT. WAREHOUSE—CONTINUOUS

Cobb and Arthur drag Fischer and Browning to the van–

> FISCHER
>
> We're worth much more to you alive...

Arthur places Fischer on the back seat– uses a DROPPER to drop LIQUID
onto Fischer's mask– his head SLUMPS FORWARDS. "Browning" yanks
the sack from his head– it is now EAMES.

> EAMES
> (excited)
> His relationship with his father's much worse
> than we thought.

> ARTHUR
> That helps us?

Arthur pulls a SNIPER RIFLE from a case by the van.

> COBB
> The stronger the issues, the more powerful the
> catharsis.

Cobb motions for Yusuf to follow him upstairs.

> ARTHUR
> But how do you reconcile them if they're that
> estranged?

> EAMES
> I'm working on that.

Arthur lines up a shot through the window–

> ARTHUR
> Well, work fast—Fischer's projections are clos-
> ing in quick, we need to break out of here
> before we're totally boxed in...

Arthur SHOOTS two snipers. Cobb and Yusuf gently load Saito into the van. He groans. Ariadne straps him in, checks his bandages. Arthur can't get the last sniper– he's too hidden behind a wall–

> EAMES
> Shouldn't be afraid to dream a little bigger,
> Arthur—

Eames lines up a shot with a grenade launcher. Fires– the sniper EXPLODES into the air– Arthur looks at Eames.

> EAMES
> Shall we?

They climb into the van–

INT./EXT. VAN ON RAINY STREETS—CONTINUOUS

The van pulls out onto the rain-drenched streets. Arthur opens the mechanism case and hands out tubes–

> COBB
>
> Shifting Fischer's antipathy from his father onto Browning should work.

> EAMES
>
> We need the imagery, the words...

> ARIADNE
>
> So you destroy his one positive relationship?

> COBB
>
> No. We repair his relationship with his father and expose his godfather's true nature.

> EAMES
>
> Hell, we should be charging Fischer as much as Saito.

> ARTHUR
>
> What about his security? It's going to get worse as we go deeper.

> COBB
>
> We bring in Mr. Charles.

> ARTHUR
>
> No.

> EAMES
>
> Who's Mr. Charles?

> ARTHUR
>
> A bad idea.

> COBB
>
> Arthur, the second we approach Fischer in that hotel, they're gonna mow us down—we run with Mr. Charles like on the Stein job.

> EAMES
>
> So you've done it before?

ARTHUR

Sure. But it didn't work. The subject realized he
was dreaming and his subconscious tore us to
pieces.

Eames takes this in.

EAMES

You learned a lot, though. Right?

COBB

(to Eames)

I'll need a decoy.

EAMES

No problem. How about a pretty young lady I've
used before?

COBB

Fine—

Cobb looks back: a second s.u.v. pulls out, tailing them.

COBB

(to Yusuf)

I know you've got to stay ahead of them, but
drive with kid gloves, okay? The world down
there is going to be very unstable—

ARTHUR

And don't make the jump too soon—that kick is
our only way back, we have to be ready to catch
it—

YUSUF

I'll use the music to let you know when it's coming, but the rest is up to you.

Arthur puts the mechanism onto the front seat.

YUSUF

Everyone ready?

Nods all round.

                              YUSUF
            Sweet dreams—

Yusuf hits a button, and we–

                                                              CUT TO:

INT. HOTEL LOBBY BAR—SUNSET

Fischer nurses a drink. Staring at the ice cracking.

                          BLONDE (O.S.)
            Am I boring you?

Fischer looks up. A beautiful BLONDE is next to him.

                              BLONDE
            I was telling you my story. I guess it wasn't to
            your liking.

                             FISCHER
            I have a lot on my mind.

Fischer looks around the bar. There are several STERN-LOOKING CHAR-
ACTERS paying him too much attention.

INT. HOTEL LOBBY—CONTINUOUS

Arthur and Ariadne sit at a table across the lobby. They spot Cobb
moving across the lobby towards Fischer.

                             ARTHUR
            And there goes Mr. Charles...

                            ARIADNE
            Who or what, exactly, is Mr. Charles?

                             ARTHUR
            It's a gambit designed to turn Fischer against
            his own subconscious.

INT. HOTEL LOBBY BAR—CONTINUOUS

Cobb approaches the bar, watched closely by Fischer's Sub-security.

> COBB
> Mr. Fischer! Good to see you again. Rod Green,
> Marketing.
> > (to Blonde)
> And you must be...

> BLONDE
> Leaving.

She presses against Fischer as she slides off her stool and deposits a cocktail napkin in front of him.

> BLONDE
> In case you get bored.

Cobb watches her walk away. The Sub-security FOLLOWS her.

> COBB
> I think you just got blown off... unless her
> phone number really does have only six digits.

Fischer glances at the napkin: "528-491."

INT. HOTEL LOBBY—CONTINUOUS

Arthur watches the Sub-security follow the Blonde.

> ARIADNE
> And why don't you approve?

> ARTHUR
> Because it involves telling the mark that he's
> dreaming. Which involves attracting a lot of
> attention to us.

> ARIADNE
> Didn't Cobb say never to do that?

> ARTHUR
> You must've noticed by now how much time
> Cobb spends doing things he says never to do.

INT. HOTEL LOBBY BAR—CONTINUOUS

Cobb turns to Fischer.

> COBB
>
> Strange way to make friends.
> (off look)
> Lifting your wallet, I mean.

Fischer pats his pocket. Empty. He looks to the lobby where he sees the Sub-security trailing the Blonde.

> FISCHER
>
> Goddamn it. The wallet alone's worth—

> COBB
>
> Five hundred bucks. I know. Don't worry, my guys are on it.

> FISCHER
>
> Who did you say you were?

Fischer looks at him, curious. Cobb plows on, confident-

> COBB
>
> I *said* I was Rod Green from Marketing—but I'm not. My name is Mr. Charles. I might seem familiar to you. I'm in charge of your security here.

INT. HOTEL LOBBY—CONTINUOUS

The Blonde hurries up to Saito, emerging from the elevator–

> BLONDE
>
> Mr. Saito, can I have a minute?

She pushes him back into the elevator, closing the door as the Sub-security approaches...

INT. ELEVATOR—CONTINUOUS

The Blonde fondles Saito's lapels, getting close.

> SAITO
>
> I'm sorry, but...

Saito glances over her shoulder to see, in the tunnel of infinite reflections created by the elevator's opposing mirrors, three reflections in, THE BLONDE IS EAMES. He winks.

> SAITO
> (pushing him away)
> Very amusing, Mr. Eames.

> EAMES
> You look a bit perkier.

A SHUDDER ripples through the elevator.

> SAITO
> Turbulence on the plane?

> EAMES
> Feels closer. That's Yusuf's driving.

And we—

CUT TO:

INT./EXT. VAN ON RAINY DOWNTOWN STREETS—DAY

Yusuf FIGHTS the wheel as the van CUTS DOWN AN ALLEY, BUMPING OVER POTHOLES and SMASHING TRASH CANS aside— THREE S.U.V.'s IN FURIOUS PURSUIT. Yusuf looks in the rear view mirror, FRUSTRATED. He checks his WATCH, then checks the back: the SLEEPERS SHAKE with the impact and we—

CUT TO:

INT. HOTEL LOBBY BAR—NIGHT

As a TREMOR echoes through the bar Fischer looks at Cobb trying to place him.

> FISCHER
> Security? You work for the hotel?

> COBB
> No. My specialty is subconscious security.

> FISCHER
> You're talking about dreams. You're talking about extraction.

> COBB
> Exactly. My job is to protect you...

Behind Fischer a WAITER puts down a tray– tipping a champagne glass over– SMASH– Cobb NOTICES. Pauses, looks across the bar– HIS TWO CHILDREN ARE CROUCHED, BACKS TOWARDS US...

Cobb looks around the bar, the patrons start to STARE at Cobb, suspicious– Cobb shifts back to Fischer–

> COBB
> My job is to protect you from any attempt to
> access your mind through your dreams.

Cobb regains his patter– the patrons lose interest...

INT. ELEVATOR—CONTINUOUS

Eames pulls out Fischer's wallet, moves to hand it to Saito, then PAUSES, opens it, leafs past the cash to find... The SNAPSHOT: young Robert holding his HOMEMADE PINWHEEL, his father blowing on it. The elevator doors open and Eames steps off. HANDS Saito the wallet.

> EAMES
> Get off at a different floor and keep moving.
> Dump the wallet, then meet me in the lobby.
> The security will try to track it down. We need
> to buy Cobb a little more time.

The doors close. Saito puts the wallet in his pocket. He COUGHS– a deep, nasty cough.

INT. HOTEL LOBBY BAR—CONTINUOUS

Cobb looks over Fischer's shoulder to see a SUITED MAN watching him. Another MAN is walking in from the lobby.

> COBB
> You're not safe here.

Cobb steps away from the bar. Fischer does not move.

> COBB
> Trust me. They're coming for you.

Fischer sizes him up, A CLAP OF THUNDER echoes, and we–

CUT TO:

INT./EXT. VAN ON RAINY DOWNTOWN STREETS—DAY

GUNSHOTS BLAST out the rear and side windows of the van– a Security Man is leaning out of the lead S.U.V. with a SHOTGUN–

WIND AND RAIN RIP THROUGH THE VAN– in the back, ARTHUR'S SLEEP-ING FACE IS WHIPPED BY THE SPRAY, AND WE–

CUT TO:

INT. HOTEL LOBBY BAR—SUNSET

Fischer looks out the windows at sudden, HURRICANE-LIKE RAIN–

> COBB
> Strange weather, huh?

A TREMOR runs through the bar– Cobb looks around–

> COBB
> You feel that?

INT. HOTEL LOBBY—CONTINUOUS

Ariadne and Arthur watch the GUSTS OF WIND RATTLE the windows. Arthur sees HOTEL GUESTS staring out at the weather, PUZZLED. Several of them TURN TO LOOK DIRECTLY AT ARTHUR.

> ARIADNE
> What's happening?

> ARTHUR
> Cobb's drawing Fischer's attention to the
> strangeness of the dream. That's making his
> subconscious look for the dreamer. For me.

And we–

CUT TO:

INT./EXT. VAN ON RAINY STREETS—DAY

At the end of the alley– Yusuf THROWS the van into a HARD RIGHT TURN– we move into EXTREME SLOW MOTION... THE SLEEPERS IN THE BACK ARE DRAWN TO ONE SIDE OF THE VAN BY THE CENTRIFUGAL FORCE... and we–

CUT TO:

INT. HOTEL LOBBY BAR—CONTINUOUS

The liquid in Fischer's drink RISES UP AGAINST ONE SIDE OF THE GLASS— Fischer notices, confused.

> **COBB**
> Very odd—the weather, the *gravity*...

Fischer looks around the bar– it's as if THE ENTIRE ROOM IS SET AT A 45-DEGREE ANGLE– glasses SLIDING off tables...

> **COBB**
> But I can explain all this. You've actually been trained for this.
> (Fischer nods)
> Think of the strangeness of the weather, the shifts in gravity.

> **COBB**
> None of this is real...
> (beat)
> We're in a dream.

Fischer looks at the room around them. Back to Cobb. All through the bar, patrons turn to look at Cobb IN UNISON.

> **COBB**
> The simplest test of what I'm saying is for you to try and remember anything about the way you arrived in this hotel... okay?

Fischer stares at Cobb, trying to process this. All around them, people STARE at Cobb. Several get up as if to approach.

> **COBB**
> Breathe. Remember the training. Accept the fact that we're in a dream. That's why I'm here pro-tecting you.

As Fischer considers this we–

CUT TO:

INT./EXT. VAN ON RAINY STREETS—DAY

Yusuf STRAIGHTENS UP the van, RACING down the street, swerving through traffic and we–

CUT TO:

INT. HOTEL LOBBY BAR—EVENING

The building gradually EASES BACK INTO ALIGNMENT–

> FISCHER
> So *you...* you're not real?

The bar patrons start to ignore Cobb again.

> COBB
> No. I'm a projection of your subconscious. I was
> put in place to protect you in the event that
> extractors pulled you into a dream. I believe
> that's what has happened.

Fischer takes this in. Then looks at the Security Men approaching across the crooked floor, he nods at Cobb–

INT. HOTEL LOBBY—EVENING

Cobb escorts Fischer across the lobby. As he does so, he walks past the two CHILDREN, backs to us– Cobb ignores them– The two Sub-security fall in behind. Cobb hurries Fischer up the stairs– then PUSHES him into–

INT. HOTEL LOBBY BATHROOM—CONTINUOUS

Fischer stumbles in– turns to Cobb, angry–

> FISCHER
> Hey—

Cobb reaches into his jacket– the First Man BURSTS in– Cobb KICKS him to the ground– DRAWS his gun as the SECOND MAN comes through the door, moving towards Fischer–

BLAM! Cobb BLASTS the Second Man in the back– TURNS and SHOOTS the First Man.

> **FISCHER**
> Jesus Christ! What are you doing?!

Cobb turns to Fischer, calm. Convincing.

> **COBB**
> Look at the gun in his hand.

Fischer looks: the Second Man was holding a pistol. Cobb opens the First Man's jacket to show Fischer his holster and sidearm.

> **COBB**
> These men were sent to abduct you.

Cobb pulls out the gun and HANDS it to Fischer.

> **COBB**
> If I'm going to help you, I need you to be calm.

Fischer remembers something.

> **FISCHER**
> If this is a dream, I have to kill myself and wake up—

Fischer raises the gun towards his head–

> **COBB**
> I wouldn't do that—they've probably got you sedated. If you pull that trigger, you might not wake up, you might drop into a lower dream state. Mr. Fischer, you know all this, you just have to remember it...

Fischer lowers the gun.

INT. HOTEL CORRIDOR—CONTINUOUS

Saito walks down the corridor, followed by a Security Man. Saito DUCKS around the corner, moves to a GARBAGE CHUTE and DROPS Fischer's WALLET into it. He SLIPS into the stairwell as the Security Man comes abreast of the chute and pauses.

INT. HOTEL CORRIDOR—CONTINUOUS

Arthur leads Ariadne to a particular room: 491.

INT. ROOM 491—CONTINUOUS

Arthur leads Ariadne in. He opens the closet, opens the room safe, pulls out FOUR BRICKS OF PLASTIC EXPLOSIVE.

> ARTHUR
> So, if everything's correct, this room should be directly below 528.

INT. HOTEL LOBBY BATHROOM—CONTINUOUS

Cobb looks reassuringly at Fischer.

> COBB
> What do you remember from before this dream?

> FISCHER
> (thinking)
> Rain... gunfire... *Uncle Peter.*
> (looks up)
> Christ—we've been kidnapped.

> COBB
> Where were they holding you?

> FISCHER
> They had us... in the back of a van...

> COBB
> Your body's bouncing around in the back of a van right now—that explains the gravity shifts.

> FISCHER
> It was... to do with a safe... Christ, why's it so hard to remember?

> COBB
> It's like trying to remember a dream after you've woken up. It takes years of practice to do it easily. So, you and Browning have been pulled into this dream so they can steal something from your mind. What?

FISCHER

They wanted a combination to a safe... they demanded the first numbers to pop into my head.

COBB

That's them extracting a locator.

FISCHER

A locator?

COBB

A number from your own subconscious. It can be used any number of ways...
(thinking)
This is a hotel. *Room numbers.* What was the number you gave them?

FISCHER

5, 2... something... it was a long number. 528... 528, 4 something.

COBB
(opens phone)
Well, we know where to start.
(into phone)
Fifth floor.

INT. ROOM 491—CONTINUOUS

Arthur hangs up the phone. He is standing on a chair, attaching the explosives to the ceiling.

ARIADNE

Do you use a timer?

ARTHUR

No, I have to judge it myself. Once you're all asleep up in room 528, I wait 'til Yusuf starts his kick...

ARIADNE

How will you know?

ARTHUR

His music warns me it's coming, then the van
hitting the barrier of the bridge should be
unmistakable—that's when I blow the floor out
from underneath us and we get a nice synchronized kick. Too soon, and we won't get pulled
out; too late and I won't be able to drop us.

ARIADNE

Why not?

ARTHUR

The van will be in free fall. I can't drop us with
no gravity.

Arthur finishes setting the charges.

INT. HOTEL LOBBY—CONTINUOUS

Saito moves through the lobby. Browning is coming in the other direction. Saito assumes him to be Eames.

SAITO

I see you've changed.

BROWNING

I'm sorry?

Eames comes up behind Browning, catching Saito's eye.

SAITO

I'm... I mistook you for a friend.

BROWNING

Good-looking fellow, I'm sure.

Browning moves off. Saito approaches Eames.

EAMES

That's Fischer's projection of Browning. We'll
keep an eye on how he behaves—

SAITO

Why?

> EAMES
>
> How he acts will tell us if Fischer's starting to suspect his motives the way we want him to.

INT. HOTEL CORRIDOR, FIFTH FLOOR—MOMENTS LATER

Cobb leads Fischer around a corner. Arthur and Ariadne are waiting in the corridor.

> COBB
>
> They work for me.

Fischer starts looking at room numbers. Stops at 528. Cobb draws his gun, steps back from the door and KICKS it open–

INT. ROOM 528—CONTINUOUS

Cobb JUMPS into the room, gun up. The room is empty. Arthur and Ariadne search the room. Saito and Eames arrive. Eames shuts the door. Arthur FINDS something–

> ARTHUR
>
> Mr. Charles!

Arthur holds up a MECHANISM CASE. Cobb shows it to Fischer.

> COBB
>
> You know what this is?

Fischer's eyes roam over the dials and plungers.

> FISCHER
>
> I think so. But I don't understand.

> COBB
>
> They were going to put you under.

> FISCHER
>
> I'm already under.

> COBB
>
> Under *again*.

> FISCHER
>
> A dream within a dream?

> ARTHUR

Shhhh!

Arthur is at the door. Someone is there. A key goes into the lock– the door starts to open– Arthur REACHES OVER and GRABS the person entering, THROWS THEM TO THE FLOOR– puts his gun in their face. IT IS BROWNING.

Fischer stares, disbelieving, at his godfather.

> FISCHER

Uncle Peter. What's going on?

Cobb pulls the key from Browning's hand: ROOM 528

> COBB

You said you were kidnapped together?

> FISCHER

Not exactly, they already had him. They'd been torturing him...

> COBB

You *saw* them torture him?

Fischer shakes his head. Looks at Browning. Thinking.

> FISCHER

The kidnappers are working for you.

> BROWNING

No, Robert—

> FISCHER

You're trying to get that safe open. To get the alternate will.

Browning looks up at Fischer.

> BROWNING

Fischer Morrow's been my entire life. I can't let you destroy it.

> FISCHER

I'm not going to throw away my inheritance. Why would I?

> BROWNING
>
> I couldn't take the chance of you rising to your father's final taunt.

> FISCHER
>
> What taunt?

> BROWNING
>
> That will. I'm sorry, Robert, but it's his final insult. A challenge to build something for yourself. He's telling you that you aren't worthy of his achievements.

Fischer takes this in. Devastated.

> FISCHER
>
> That he was "disappointed?"

> BROWNING
>
> I'm so sorry. But he was wrong. You'll make his company even greater than he ever could.

> COBB
>
> Your godfather's lying, Robert.

Fischer turns to Cobb.

> FISCHER
>
> How do you know?

> COBB
>
> It's what I do. He's hiding something.

Cobb looks at Browning.

> COBB
>
> Let's find out what.

Cobb nods at Arthur, who starts unpacking the mechanism. Browning watches. Silent.

> COBB
>
> Let's do to him what he was going to do to you.

Cobb rolls up his sleeve. Nods at Fischer to do the same.

                          COBB
    We'll penetrate his subconscious and find out
    what he doesn't want you to know.

Fischer looks Cobb in the eye. Decides– rolls up his sleeve, offering
his bare arm. The team run tubes to each other– Arthur injects Fischer,
whose head slumps.

                         ARTHUR
    He's out.

                        ARIADNE
    Wait, Cobb—I'm lost. Whose subconscious are
    we going into?

                          COBB
    Fischer's. I told him it was Browning's so he'd
    come with us as part of our team.

                         ARTHUR
                       (impressed)
    He's going to help us break into his own sub-
    conscious.

                          COBB
    That's the idea. He'll think that his security is
    Browning's and fight them to learn the truth
    about his father.

Arthur hits buttons on the mechanism. The team goes out one by one.
Cobb is last.

                          COBB
    Fischer's subconscious is going to run you
    down hard.

                         ARTHUR
    I'll lead them on a merry chase.

                          COBB
    Be back in time for the kick.

                         ARTHUR
    I'm on it.

Cobb is no longer listening– he stares at the net curtains, BILLOWING like those in Mal's suite– a GLIMPSE of someone (Mal?) as the screen goes WHITE, and we are–

EXT. SNOW-COVERED MOUNTAINS—DAY

CLOSE ON Cobb's face, staring. Fixed.

>   ARIADNE (O.S.)
> Cobb? Cobb?

Ariadne is beside him. They stand on a cliff, dressed in white snowsuits, carrying white-painted weapons like WWII commandos. Cobb checks his SNIPER RIFLE, examines their objective: a massive FORTIFIED MEDICAL FACILITY a mile below.

>   ARIADNE
> What's down there?

>   COBB
> Hopefully, the truth we want Fischer to learn.

>   ARIADNE
> I meant what's down there for you?

Cobb turns to her. Eames, Saito and Fischer arrive, SKIING down from the hill above. Cobb pulls Eames out of Fischer's earshot.

>   COBB
> You're the dreamer. I need you to draw the secu-
> rity away from the complex.

>   EAMES
> Then who guides Fischer in? You?

>   COBB
> If I know the route... we could be compromised.

Eames looks at Cobb, uneasy. Ariadne comes over.

>   ARIADNE
> I designed the place.

>   COBB
> No. You're with me.

THEY STAND ON A CLIFF, DRESSED IN WHITE SNOWSUITS, CARRYING
WHITE-PAINTED WEAPONS LIKE WWII COMMANDOS.

3

176-4

176-7

SAITO COUGH

176-8

SPECKS OF
BLOOD IN
THE SNOW.

40

SCENE #184

184-1A

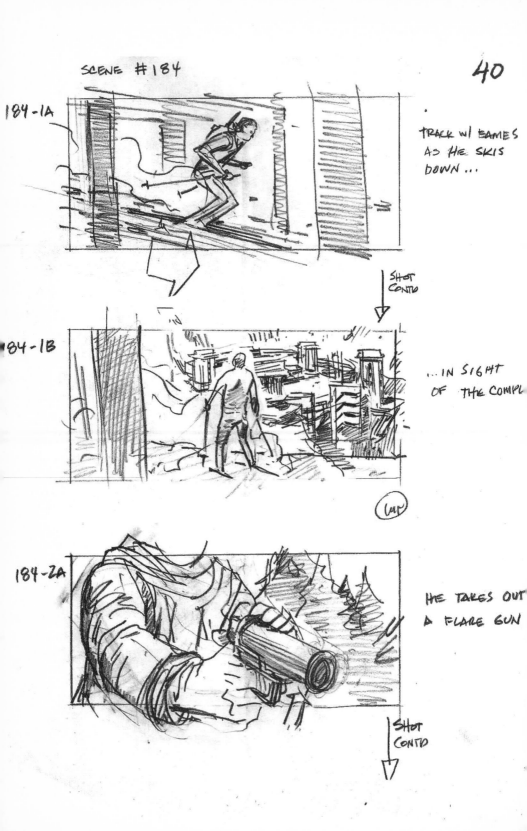

TRACK w/ EAMES
AS HE SKIS
DOWN ...

SHOT
CONT'D

184-1B

... IN SIGHT
OF THE COMPL

184-2A

HE TAKES OUT
A FLARE GUN

SHOT
CONT'D

41

-2B

TILT UP W/ IT
HE FIRES,

TILT
UP

CUT

SCENE # 185

-1

SECURITY
GUARDS ON
RAMPART SPOT
FLARE.

CUT

-2A

PATROLS ARE
SENT OUT TO
INVESTIGATE.

SHOT
CONT'D

42

185-2B

SCENE # 186

186-3A

OVER EAMES
TO GUARDS

SHOT
CONT'D

186-3B

EAMES

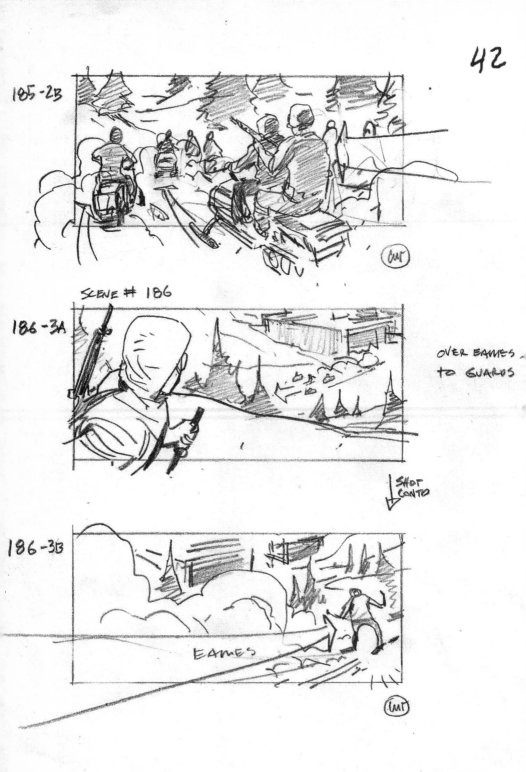

SKI SEQUENCE 11/09/09

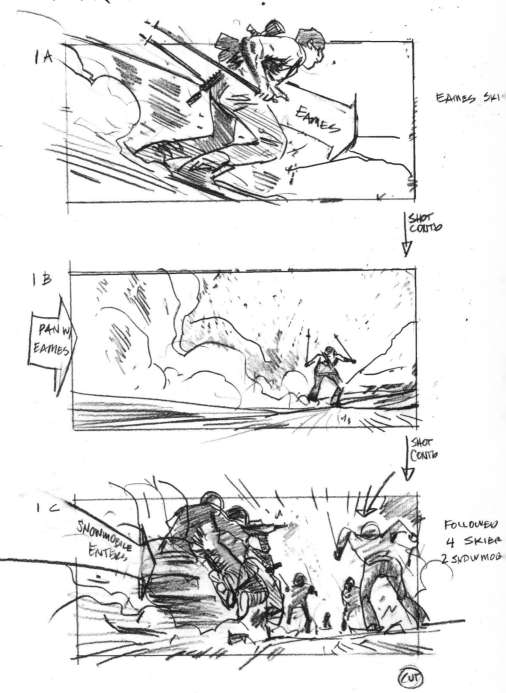

2

CUT

3

HE TURNS +
FIRES.

CUT

4

1ST SECURITY
SKIER IS
SHOT..

CUT

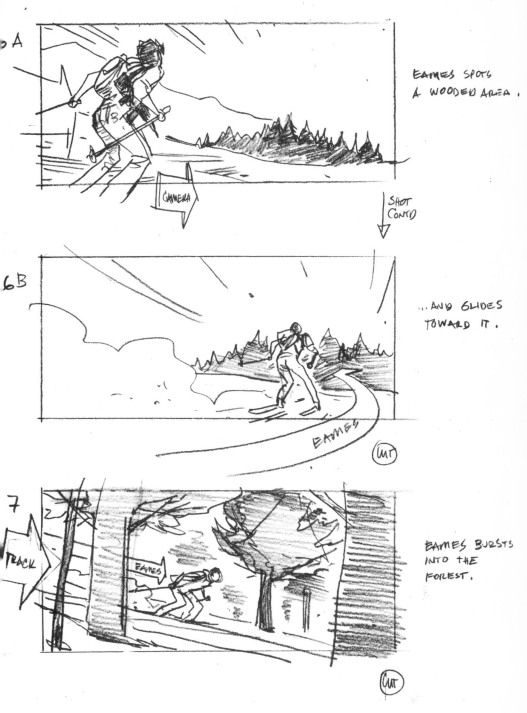

A

EAMES SPOTS
A WOODED AREA.

CAMERA

SHOT
CONT'D

6 B

...AND GLIDES
TOWARD IT.

EAMES

(CUT)

7

TRACK

EAMES

EAMES BURSTS
INTO THE
FOREST.

CUT

SC. # 189

89-1 A

COBB + ARIAD
SKI —

SHOT
CONT'D

189-1 B

- STOP -

SHOT
CONT'D

189-1C

LISTEN —
THE WIND SOUN
UNUSUALLY LOW

(MT)

SAITO (O.S.)
I could do it.

They turn to Saito. Saito shrugs at Eames. Eames smiles.

COBB
Eames, brief Saito on the route into the complex.
What we're looking for is going to be in the
most heavily fortified section. That north tower.

Cobb moves to Fischer. Saito COUGHS. SPITS. Eames sees BLOOD on the snow. Looks at Saito.

COBB
Mr. Fischer, you're going in with Saito.

FISCHER
You're not coming in?

COBB
You have to do this on your own. You have to
get in there, break into your godfather's mind
and find out the truth about your father.

Cobb taps Fischer's radio mike.

COBB
Keep this live at all times. I'll be listening in,
covering you.
(holds up the sniper rifle)
The windows on the upper floors are big
enough that I can cover you from that south
tower.

Cobb slips into his skis, shoulders his rifle.

CUT TO:

INT. ROOM 528—NIGHT

Arthur checks the mechanism. He hears LOW BOOMS like thunder. He
checks his watch- THE SECOND HAND CRAWLS FORWARDS. With a last
look at the sleepers, he heads out into the corridor...

INT./EXT. VAN ON RAINY DOWNTOWN STREETS—DAY

A GUNSHOT slams into the van as Yusuf DRIVES– he glances back to see a MOTORCYCLE pulling up behind him, the REAR PASSENGER FIRING A SHOTGUN– the bike pulls alongside Yusuf's window as the passenger RELOADS– Yusuf YANKS the wheel TOWARDS the bike, bringing the shotgun barrel into the cab so he can GRAB it, spin the wheel back– PULLING the passenger from the back of the bike... Yusuf turns a corner, heading into a disused MARKET–

INT. HOTEL CORRIDOR—CONTINUOUS

Arthur walks towards the elevator. It OPENS– a SECURITY MAN emerges, heading right for him. Arthur takes a TURN, speeding up. The BOOMS are louder, and we–

CUT TO:

INT./EXT. VAN ON RAINY DOWNTOWN STREETS—DAY

The bike crosses behind the van, catching up again as the driver pulls a handgun and starts BLASTING. Up ahead, an S.U.V. sits in a side road, lining up to head off the van– the SECURITY MAN driving the S.U.V. guns it, as the bike creeps up on the other side of the van– Yusuf HITS THE BRAKES, forcing the bike out into the path of the S.U.V.– BAM– the bike SPINS off the front corner of the S.U.V., tossing the rider like a rag doll–

Heading out of the market, the van races onto a FREEWAY ON RAMP, approaching the BRIDGE. An S.U.V. SMASHES into the van's side, FORCING it up against a CRASH BARRIER... the van starts to SLOWLY TILT OVER THE BARRIER as the S.U.V. PUSHES–

CUT TO:

INT. HOTEL CORRIDOR—NIGHT

As Arthur hurries down the corridor, the corridor starts to TILT, and Arthur is forced to run UP ONTO THE WALL– he rounds a corner– STRAIGHT INTO another Security Man– Arthur HEAD BUTTS him and they STRUGGLE– as they struggle, the corridor SPINS around, THROWING THEM UP ONTO THE WALLS, THE CEILING– as wall becomes floor they DROP through a door into–

INT. HOTEL ROOM—CONTINUOUS

The fight continues all over the spinning room- and we-

CUT TO:

INT./EXT. VAN ON RAINY OFF RAMP NEAR BRIDGE—DAY

SLEEPING ARTHUR BOUNCES around as the van TILTS, SCRAPING along the barrier- the van CLEARS THE END OF THE BARRIER AND ROLLS DOWN THE EMBANKMENT, and we-

CUT TO:

INT. HOTEL ROOM—NIGHT

Arthur and the Security Man DROP to the floor, Arthur on top. Arthur gets up- heads to the stairwell.

INT./EXT. VAN ON RAINY STREET NEAR BRIDGE—DAY

The van SETTLES with a thump. Yusuf BREATHES hard. Then SMILES as he realizes he is in one piece. A RINGING BELL up ahead makes him look up to the bridge, where the barriers are starting to come down. Yusuf checks his watch-

> **YUSUF**
> Bugger.

Yusuf hits the gas, heading for the bridge. An S.U.V. lines up behind him, trying to catch up before the van crosses the barrier onto the bridge-

The van JUST MAKES IT- the S.U.V. behind RIPS its rear axle off, SCRAPING to a halt on the rising section. The Security Man inside starts FIRING on the van...

INT. HOTEL STAIRWELL—CONTINUOUS

Arthur RACES down the steps- OPENS the door to the fourth floor- spots SECURITY MEN outside room 491.

> **ARTHUR**
> Hey!

They TURN- he DARTS back into the stairwell- RACES down the stairs- the Security Men follow- they start SHOOTING, and we-

CUT TO:

EXT. SNOW-COVERED MOUNTAINS—DAY

Eames SKIS down within sight of the hospital complex. He reaches into his pack and lets off a FLARE.

EXT. HOSPITAL COMPLEX—CONTINUOUS

Security Men on the ramparts spot the flare and send PATROLS out on skis and SNOWMOBILES to investigate.

EXT. SNOW-COVERED MOUNTAINS—CONTINUOUS

Eames watches them close in, then launches himself down the mountain, STREAKING across the icy slope, and we–

CUT TO:

INT./EXT. VAN ON RAINY RISING BRIDGE—DAY

Yusuf PULLS FORWARDS, looking over his shoulder to line up a BACKWARDS RUN at the edge. He DUCKS as vicious FIRE from the S.U.V. HAMMERS the vehicle. He looks at his watch. The SECOND HAND TICKING SLOWLY...

                    YUSUF
          Sod it. I hope you're ready.

He grabs an MP3 player and reaches into the back to place HEADPHONES on sleeping Arthur's head. As he does so, he notices Saito's bandage BLEEDING THROUGH. Yusuf hits PLAY– Edith Piaf's "Non, je ne regrette rien" starts up and we–

CUT TO:

INT. HOTEL STAIRWELL—NIGHT

Arthur STOPS, hearing something– MASSIVE LOW-END MUSICAL TONES– he looks up PANICKED–

                    ARTHUR
          No, Yusuf. Too soon!

SHOTS slam into the stairs around him and we–

CUT TO:

EXT. SNOW-COVERED MOUNTAINS—DAY

Cobb and Ariadne make their way down towards the complex.

> **EAMES (over radio)**
> *Cobb? Are you hearing that?*

Cobb listens. The wind sounds unusually LOW.

EXT. FOREST, SNOW-COVERED MOUNTAINS—CONTINUOUS

Eames is hidden at the base of some trees, whispering as a patrol passes beneath his position.

> **EAMES**
> I noticed it twenty minutes ago—at first I
> thought it was just wind...

EXT. SNOW-COVERED MOUNTAINS—CONTINUOUS

Cobb is listening intently. The "wind" changes pitch.

> **COBB**
> No, it's music. Dammit.

> **EAMES (over radio)**
> *What do we do?*

> **COBB**
> We move fast. Saito, did you copy?

EXT. MOUNTAINS, THE OTHER SIDE OF THE COMPLEX—CONTINUOUS

Saito and Fischer CLIMB down a CLIFF FACE above the complex–

> **SAITO**
> We're going as fast as we can.

EXT. SNOW-COVERED MOUNTAINS—CONTINUOUS

Ariadne looks at Cobb, concerned.

> **ARIADNE**
> How long do we have?

> COBB
>
> Yusuf's about ten seconds from the jump, which gives Arthur about three minutes, which gives us about—

> ARIADNE
>
> Sixty minutes.

> COBB
>
> The route you gave them, can they do it in under an hour?

> ARIADNE
>
> I don't think so. They've still got to climb down to the middle terrace.

> COBB
>
> They need a new route—a direct route.

> ARIADNE
>
> The building's designed as a labyrinth.

> COBB
>
> There must be access routes that cut through the maze.
> (into radio)
> Eames?

EXT. FOREST, SNOW-COVERED MOUNTAINS—CONTINUOUS

Eames cannot answer– he SLALOMS through the forest, Sub-security in hot pursuit, bullets smashing into the trunks...

EXT. SNOW-COVERED MOUNTAINS—CONTINUOUS

Cobb turns to Ariadne.

> COBB
>
> Did Eames add any features?

> ARIADNE
>
> Yes.

> COBB
>
> What did he add?

Ariadne looks at Cobb.

> ARIADNE
> I shouldn't tell you. If Mal—

> COBB
> There's no time—what did he add?

> ARIADNE
> Utility closets, trap doors...

> COBB
> What about service features? Did he add any
> large pipes or—

> ARIADNE
> Ducts. He added an air duct system—it doesn't
> follow the maze. They can use it to go straight
> from the outer walls to the upper tower.

> COBB
> Explain it to them.

> ARIADNE
> (into radio)
> Saito?

EXT. CLIFF FACE BEHIND COMPLEX—CONTINUOUS

Saito is using a hammer to tap in a belay.

> SAITO
> Go ahead.

And we–

                                                    CUT TO:

INT./EXT. VAN ON RAINY RAISED BRIDGE—DAY

Yusuf looks at the Security Man in the s.u.v., gives him the finger and
hits the GAS– RACING BACKWARDS at the barrier... and we–

CUT TO:

INT. HOTEL STAIRWELL—NIGHT

Arthur RUNS UP the stairs, gun in hand– rounds a corner and– IMPOS-
SIBLY– arrives behind the Security Man– who looks at him, CONFUSED,
then looks down to realize he is now at the edge of a dangerous drop–
Arthur shrugs.

                         ARTHUR
            Paradox.

Arthur PUSHES him over the edge– he falls– Arthur races up to the
fourth floor– throws open the door– and we–

CUT TO:

INT./EXT. VAN ON RAINY RAISED BRIDGE—DAY

In SLOW MOTION– the van SMASHES THROUGH THE CONCRETE BAR-
RIER– and we–

CUT TO:

INT. HOTEL CORRIDOR—NIGHT

Arthur is SPRINTING down the corridor when a TREMENDOUS CRASH
sends him FLYING into the air– and we–

CUT TO:

EXT. SNOW-COVERED MOUNTAINS—DAY

A MASSIVE RUMBLE prompts Cobb to look across the valley–

EXT. FOREST, SNOW-COVERED MOUNTAINS—CONTINUOUS

Eames shoots out of the trees, then FALLS to the snow as he sees a great
CRACKING up ahead– the SLOPE IS FALLING AWAY IN AN AVALANCHE–

EXT. CLIFF FACE BEHIND COMPLEX—CONTINUOUS

Saito hears the RUMBLE above them. He looks down, Fischer is below,
near the bottom of the sheer face–

                         SAITO
            Look out!

Saito CUTS the rope– they FALL– HIT the icy face and SLIDE down the slope, clearing the path of the avalanche– and we–

                                                                    CUT TO:

INT./EXT. VAN—DAY

In EXTREME SLOW MOTION, the van emerges from the concrete balustrade and starts FALLING– and we–

                                                                    CUT TO:

INT. HOTEL CORRIDOR—NIGHT

Arthur is still FLYING through the corridor, NOT LANDING– GRAVITY HAS DISAPPEARED... he scrambles for a handhold, GRABBING a sconce– and we–

                                                                    CUT TO:

EXT. SNOW-COVERED MOUNTAINS—DAY

Cobb watches the avalanche cloud slide past the complex.

                          ARIADNE
          What was *that*?

                            COBB
          The kick.

                    EAMES (over radio)
          Cobb? Did we miss it?

                            COBB
          Yeah, we missed it.

EXT. FOREST, SNOW-COVERED MOUNTAINS—CONTINUOUS

Eames is lying on the snow.

                           EAMES
          What the hell do we do now?

                    COBB (over radio)
          Finish the job before the next kick.

> EAMES

What next kick?

EXT. SNOW-COVERED MOUNTAINS—CONTINUOUS

Cobb looks at Ariadne as he talks into the radio.

> COBB

When the van hits the water. I figure Arthur's got a couple minutes and we've got about twenty.

Cobb and Ariadne MOVE towards the base of the complex.

EXT. HOSPITAL COMPLEX—CONTINUOUS

Saito and Fischer RUN around the base of the building. They find a large EXHAUST PORT. Lay a charge on the GRILL. They BLOW the charge. Climb into the open vent.

INT./EXT. VAN—DAY

In EXTREME SLOW MOTION, the van seems SUSPENDED IN MID-AIR TEN STORIES ABOVE THE RIVER... and we–

> CUT TO:

INT. HOTEL CORRIDOR—NIGHT

In ZERO GRAVITY, Arthur pulls himself to the door of 491, opens it. He looks at the charges planted on the ceiling.

> ARTHUR

How the hell do I *drop* you?

He PULLS the charges from the ceiling. Hurrying. And we–

> CUT TO:

INT. DUCT SYSTEM, HOSPITAL COMPLEX—CONTINUOUS

Saito and Fischer hurry through the duct system. Saito is falling behind, coughing up blood.

EXT. UPPER TERRACE, HOSPITAL COMPLEX—CONTINUOUS

Cobb GRABS a Security Guard from behind, strangling him uncon-
scious. He beckons to Ariadne, covering her as she runs towards him.
They enter the base of the south tower.

INT. TOP ROOM, SOUTH TOWER, HOSPITAL COMPLEX—CONTINUOUS

A guard is manning the tower. Cobb and Ariadne enter– Cobb SHOOTS
the guard and moves to the window.

> ARIADNE
> (she points)
> That's the antechamber outside the strongroom.

Cobb looks at the large windows of the antechamber.

> COBB
> What about the strongroom? Doesn't it have
> any windows?

> ARIADNE
> Wouldn't be very strong if it did.
> (off look)
> Look, if you wanted to design it yourself—

> COBB
> It's fine. Better hope that we like what Fischer
> finds in there.

Cobb sets up his sniper rifle. Through the scope he can see three
guards on the balcony outside the chamber. Three more inside.
Cobb casually picks them off with his rifle. Ariadne watches through
binoculars, appalled.

> ARIADNE
> These projections, they're parts of his subcon-
> scious?

> COBB
> Yeah.

> ARIADNE
> Are you destroying those parts of his mind?

                              COBB
              No, of course not, they're just projections.

                        EAMES (over radio)
                      Cobb? Something's wrong.

EXT. FOREST, SNOW-COVERED MOUNTAINS—CONTINUOUS

Eames is watching the patrols HEAD BACK towards the complex.

                              EAMES
              They're heading your way. Like they know
              something.

INT. TOP ROOM, SOUTH TOWER, HOSPITAL COMPLEX—CONTINUOUS

Cobb hears this. Concerned.

                              COBB
                      Buys us some time.

                        EAMES (over radio)
                          On my way.

EXT. FOREST, SNOW-COVERED MOUNTAINS—CONTINUOUS

Eames TAKES OFF towards the base of the complex. And we–

                                                          CUT TO:

INT. ROOM 528—NIGHT

Arthur FLOATS into the room. The SLEEPERS are floating, loosely connected by their tubes. Arthur looks at them, MIND RACING. He PULLS
Cobb towards Eames, and we–

                                                          CUT TO:

INT. DUCT SYSTEM, HOSPITAL COMPLEX—DAY

Saito and Fischer approach the grate covering the exit to the anteroom.
Saito SLUMPS to the floor of the duct, pulls out his radio. Fischer looks at
him– he is PALE, SHIVERING. Fischer takes the radio, WHISPERS into it.

                        FISCHER (over radio)
                We're here. Are we clear to proceed?

INT. TOP ROOM, SOUTH TOWER, HOSPITAL COMPLEX—CONTINUOUS

Cobb SCANS the anteroom through the scope—it looks clear.

> COBB
> You're clear, but hurry—there's an army headed
> your way...

Ariadne watches the patrols approaching the complex...

INT. DUCT SYSTEM, HOSPITAL COMPLEX—CONTINUOUS

The SQUELCH from the radio is too loud- Fischer GRABS it and turns
the volume to zero as he starts to remove the grate...

EXT. BASE OF THE HOSPITAL COMPLEX—CONTINUOUS

Eames is setting MINES along the LOWEST WALL of the structure. He
moves carefully- there is a SHEER DROP below the wall...

INT. TOP ROOM, SOUTH TOWER, HOSPITAL COMPLEX—CONTINUOUS

Cobb SPOTS something through his scope. Something *above* the main
windows, glimpsed through the side of the skylight.

> COBB
> Shit. There's someone else in there.

Cobb prepares to fire. Ariadne GRABS the radio–

> ARIADNE
> Fischer, stop! It's a trap!—

INT. DUCT SYSTEM, HOSPITAL COMPLEX—CONTINUOUS

Fischer does not see the flashing light on his radio as he carefully lifts
the grate. He motions for Saito to stay...

INT. TOP ROOM, SOUTH TOWER, HOSPITAL COMPLEX—CONTINUOUS

Cobb TENSES to fire...

> COBB
> Come on... a little lower... a little—

COBB FREEZES– IT IS MAL IN HIS SIGHTS. Ariadne puts up her binoculars. Spots Mal. Fischer is climbing out of the vent...

                              ARIADNE
              Cobb, that's not really her—

Cobb turns to her-

                               COBB
              How can you *know* that?

INT. ANTECHAMBER—CONTINUOUS

    Fischer moves into the antechamber, cautious...

                             FISCHER
              I'm in.

Fischer turns up the volume-

                      ARIADNE (over radio)
              Fischer, look out!—

Mal DROPS gracefully to the floor behind him-

                               MAL
              Hello.

INT. TOP ROOM, SOUTH TOWER, HOSPITAL COMPLEX—CONTINUOUS

    Cobb looks at Ariadne-

                              ARIADNE
              Cobb, she's just a projection. Fischer... he's *real.*

Cobb thinks. Nods, TURNS back to the scope- too late- MAL SHOOTS
FISCHER- Cobb reflexively pulls the trigger- Mal GOES DOWN- Cobb
steps back from the scope, STUNNED.

                              ARIADNE
              Eames? Get to the anteroom now!

They run for the door.

INT. DUCT SYSTEM, HOSPITAL COMPLEX—CONTINUOUS

    Saito STARTS as he hears the shot. He starts edging forwards, clutching
    his belly. And we-

CUT TO:

INT. ROOM 528—NIGHT

The sleepers are floating in a rough stack, top-and-tailed. Arthur pulls the bedding from the bed and uses the sheet to bind the sleepers together. And we—

CUT TO:

INT./EXT. VAN—DAY

In EXTREME SLOW MOTION, the van CREEPS DOWNWARDS, still high above the river... and we—

CUT TO:

INT. HOTEL CORRIDOR—NIGHT

Arthur PUSHES the floating stack of sleepers to the elevator. He hits the button— the doors open— he pushes them in— GRABS the charges- climbs through the hatch in the ceiling and we—

CUT TO:

INT. DUCT SYSTEM, HOSPITAL COMPLEX—DAY

Eames steps over Saito, who looks up at him with DYING eyes—

INT. ANTECHAMBER, HOSPITAL CORRIDOR—DAY

Eames jumps out of the vent to find Cobb and Ariadne standing over the bodies of Fischer and Mal.

                         EAMES
            What happened?

                        ARIADNE
            Mal killed Fischer—

                          COBB
            I wouldn't shoot her.

Eames grabs a defibrillator from the wall and pulls Fischer's jacket open—

                        COBB
            It won't do any good—

Eames SHOCKS Fischer's chest...

                        COBB
            Even if you could revive his body, his mind's
            trapped down there. It's over.

Eames listens for a pulse. Looks up at Cobb.

                        EAMES
            So that's it, then? We failed.

                        COBB
            I'm sorry.

                        EAMES
            It's you who doesn't get back to your family.

Eames looks down at Fischer. Then over to the double doors.

                        EAMES
            I wanted to know what was going to happen in
            there. I think we had this one.

                        ARIADNE
            There's still a way: We follow Fischer down—

They look at her.

                        EAMES
            We're almost out of time—

                        ARIADNE
            Down there they'll be enough time. We'll find
            him—soon as you hear Arthur's music start,
            you use the defibrillator to revive him—we give
            him his own early kick from below. Get him in
            there—
                    (points to doors)
            Then, as the music ends you blow the hospital
            and we all ride the kick back up through the
            layers.

Eames looks at her, then to Cobb.

> **EAMES**
>
> Okay, Saito can hold them off while I plant the
> rest of the charges.

> **COBB**
>
> Saito's not going to last, Eames.

> **ARIADNE**
>
> We have to try!

> **EAMES**
>
> Go for it, but I'm taking the kick whether you're
> back or not...

Eames pulls the mechanism from his pack. Offers it to Ariadne. Cobb watches. Silent. Ariadne pulls out the tubes–

> **ARIADNE**
>
> Can I trust you to do what's needed? Mal's down
> there—

> **COBB**
>
> And I can find her. She'll have Fischer.

> **ARIADNE**
>
> How do you know?

> **COBB**
>
> She wants me to come after him. She wants me
> back down there with her.

Cobb rolls his sleeve up. Ariadne rolls up her own sleeve. Eames NODS. Cobb and Ariadne lie down. Eames hits the button– WATER. BUBBLES. DROWNING. And we are–

EXT. COAST (LIMBO)—DAY

Ariadne lies in the SURF, STARING up at a CLOUDLESS SKY. A tremendous BOOM prompts her to look around her– URBAN BUILDINGS PILED right down to the water. The buildings are DECAYING, falling into the ocean like a GLACIER calving. Cobb WADES towards her through the shallow water. Ariadne looks up at the crumbling city around them.

> **ARIADNE**
>
> This is your world?

COBB
It was. And this is where she'll be.

And we–

CUT TO:

INT. ELEVATOR SHAFT—DAY

Arthur floats on top of the elevator, planting small charges on the EMERGENCY BRAKES and CABLE. He sets them, GRABS the other explosives, then PUSHES AWAY, shooting up the shaft. As he hits the DETONATOR, BLASTING the braking and safety systems of the elevator, we move into SLOW MOTION, the fireballs FLAMING OUT in graceful licks and we–

DISSOLVE TO:

INT. ANTECHAMBER—DAY

Eames RACES around, full speed– getting the defibrillator paddles– laying them by Fischer's body– he runs into the duct– pulls Saito up to a seated position and hands him a handgun.

EAMES
Come on, Saito. I need you to cover Fischer
while I plant the charges.

Saito nods weakly, tries to hold the gun. Eames moves to the window– pulls his machine gun off– checks its load. Ready. He watches the security patrols climb up the outer walls... Eames lays down a HAIL of covering fire– then heads outside–

EXT. HOSPITAL COMPLEX—CONTINUOUS

Eames races along the upper terrace dodging fire– BULLETS SHATTER a window behind him and we move into SLOW MOTION, the glass CASCADING GENTLY and we–

DISSOLVE TO:

EXT. COAST (LIMBO)— DAY

Cobb and Ariadne climb out of the waves, full speed. They move into the shadow of the tall, crumbling buildings. The streets are eerily DESERTED. As they move further in, the buildings become NEWER,

CONCEPT ART

PREVIOUS PAGE: Cube City Street Concept. ABOVE: Walking to the Skyscraper in Limbo. (Illustrations by Nathaniel West, digital paintings).

TOP LEFT: The Shoreline of Limbo. TOP RIGHT View of Limbo Beach from Elevator. BOTTOM: Utopia in Deterioration. (Illustrations by Nathaniel West, digital paintings)

ABOVE: Asleep in the Filthy Bathroom. **RIGHT, FROM TOP TO BOTTOM:**
The Japanese Castle, Japanese Castle Dining Room, Paris Workshop.
(Illustrations by Nathaniel West, except top right, by Guy H. Dyas,
digital paintings)

Paris Café Explosion. (Illustrations by Nathaniel West, digital paintings)

different. Ariadne marvels at the extraordinary collection of buildings–
every architectural style imaginable in waves of FAILED UTOPIAS.

> ARIADNE
>
> You built all this?

> COBB
>
> We both did.

> ARIADNE
>
> It's incredible.

> COBB
>
> We built for years. Then, when that got stale, we
> started in on the memories.

A child's SHOUT echoes through the deserted canyons, prompting
Cobb to look down a side street: a LITTLE BLONDE BOY crouched, his
back to us. A LITTLE BLONDE GIRL joins the boy, and, as Cobb turns
down the street, they run off.

Cobb and Ariadne emerge into a peculiar SQUARE lined with an eclec-
tic mix of buildings, from APARTMENT BLOCKS to HOUSES.

> COBB
>
> This is our neighborhood.

> ARIADNE
> (confused)
>
> From what city?

> COBB
>
> No. *Our* neighborhood.
> (pointing)
> That was our first apartment... then we moved
> to that building... we got that small house when
> Mal became pregnant.

> ARIADNE
>
> You reconstructed them all from memory?

> COBB
>
> We had time.

Cobb pauses in front of a French country house. Staring.

> ARIADNE
>
> What's that?

> COBB
>
> The house Mal grew up in.

> ARIADNE
>
> Will she be in there?

> COBB
>
> No. Come on—

Cobb leads Ariadne to the entrance of a glass skyscraper.

INT. SKYSCRAPER LOBBY (LIMBO)—CONTINUOUS

Cobb leads Ariadne across the gleaming lobby to the elevators.

> COBB
>
> We both wanted a house, but we both loved
> skyscrapers. In the real world we had to choose.
> Not here.

INT. SKYSCRAPER ELEVATOR (LIMBO)—CONTINUOUS

Cobb pulls out his handgun, and a ziplock bag full of bullets.

> ARIADNE
>
> How do we send Fischer back?

> COBB
>
> We need some kind of kick.

> ARIADNE
>
> What?

> COBB
>
> I'll improvise.

Cobb COCKS his weapon, and the ELEVATOR STOPS. The doors open. Ariadne moves to exit, Cobb stops her.

> COBB
>
> There's something you have to understand
> about me. About inception. You see, an idea is
> like a virus...

Cobb leads her out of the lift...

INT. PENTHOUSE (LIMBO)— CONTINUOUS

Cobb and Ariadne step off the lift and into the incongruous interior of a craftsman house. They cautiously move down the corridor towards the back of the house...

> COBB
> Resilient...
> > (turns to Ariadne)
> Highly contagious, and an idea can *grow*. The smallest seed of an idea can grow to define or destroy your world...

Cobb is staring into the kitchen. Mal is sitting at the table, back to them, staring out at the porch– the TOWERS of Limbo stretching off behind it.

> MAL
> The smallest idea, such as... *"Your world is not real."*

Cobb hands Ariadne his gun and moves towards Mal.

> MAL
> A simple little thought that changes *every-thing*...

Ariadne watches as Cobb sits down beside Mal. And we–

CUT TO:

INT. ELEVATOR SHAFT—NIGHT

Arthur FLIES back down the shaft to the top of the elevator, SQUEEZES past the car to the bottom and starts to set the MAIN CHARGES ACROSS THE BOTTOM OF THE CAR, and we–

CUT TO:

INT. PENTHOUSE (LIMBO)— DAY

Cobb touches Mal's arm– she TURNS, angry. It is only now that we see that she holds a CARVING KNIFE. Mal looks at Ariadne.

                              MAL
          So certain of your world. Of what's real. Do you
          think *he* is—
                    (points at Cobb)
          Or do you think he's as lost as I was?

                              COBB
          I know what's real.

                              MAL
          What *are* the distinguishing characteristics of a
          dream? Mutable laws of physics? Tell that to the
          quantum physicists. Reappearance of the dead?
          What about heaven and hell? Persecution of the
          dreamer, the creator, the messiah? They cruci-
          fied Christ, didn't they?

                              COBB
          I know what's real.

                              MAL
          No creeping doubts? Not feeling persecuted,
          Dom? Chased around the globe by anonymous
          corporations and police forces? The way the
          projections persecute the dreamer?

Mal puts her hand on his face. Pitying.

                              MAL
          Admit it, Dom. You don't believe in one reality
          anymore. So choose. Choose your reality like I
          did. Choose to be here. Choose me.

                              COBB
                        (rising anger)
          I have chosen, Mal. Our children. I have to get
          back to them. Because *you* left them. You left *us*.

                              MAL
          You're wrong, Dom. You're confused... our chil-
          dren are *here*—

A child's SHOUT draws Cobb- James CROUCHES on the porch, back to
us. Philippa joins him, also turned away. Cobb watches, moved. Mal
leans in close.

MAL
(whispers)
And you'd like to see their faces again, wouldn't
you, Dom?

COBB
Our real children are waiting for me up above.

And we–

CUT TO:

INT. ELEVATOR—NIGHT

Arthur scrambles to arrange the sleepers on the floor of the car– as his
hand comes away from Saito, he sees BLOOD on it. He looks at Saito's
belly– the blood is coming through his shirt. Arthur sticks headphones
on sleeping Eames, and we–

CUT TO:

EXT. HOSPITAL FORTRESS—DAY

Eames throws a GRENADE, blowing up the security forces trying to
ascend the terraces. He DUCKS to the ground to avoid HEAVY FIRE–
starts unpacking the charges and setting them along the base of the
terraces–

INT. DUCT SYSTEM, HOSPITAL COMPLEX—CONTINUOUS

Saito looks up as he hears a Security Guard climbing through the duct...
he raises his gun, TREMBLING with weakness... And we–

CUT TO:

INT. KITCHEN, PENTHOUSE (LIMBO)—DAY

Mal laughs at Cobb.

MAL
(laughs)
Up above? Listen to yourself. You judged me for
believing the very same thing.

Mal points at the children–

                              MAL
          These *are* our children. Watch.
                      (turns to the kids)
          Hey, James! Philippa?!

The children START TO TURN to us— BUT COBB CLOSES HIS EYES.

                              COBB
          They're not real, Mal. Our real children are wait-
          ing for us—

The children run off. Cobb opens his eyes.

                              MAL
          You keep telling yourself that but you don't
          believe it—

                              COBB
          I know it—

                              MAL
          And what if you're wrong? What if I'm what's
          real?

Cobb is silent.

                              MAL
          You keep telling yourself what you know... but
          what do you believe? What do you *feel*?

Cobb looks at Mal. Struggling.

                              COBB
          Guilt. I feel guilt. And however confused I
          might get. However lost I might seem... it's
          always there. Telling me something. Reminding
          me of the truth.

                              MAL
          What truth?

                              COBB
          That you were wrong to doubt our world. That
          the idea that drove you to question your reality
          was a lie...

                          MAL
How could you *know* it was a lie?

                          COBB
Because it was *my* lie.

                          MAL
                       (realizing)
Because you planted the idea in my mind.

                          COBB
Because I performed inception on my own wife,
then reaped the bitter rewards...

                        ARIADNE
Why?

                          COBB
We'd become lost in here. Living in a world of
infinite possibilities. A world where we were
gods. I realized we needed to escape, but she'd
locked away her knowledge of the unreality of
this world...

INSERT CUT: *Mal opens the doll's house. Takes the spinning top, lies it
down in the safe.* LOCKS IT AWAY.

                          COBB
I couldn't make Mal understand that we needed
to break free. To die. So I started to search our
world...

Cobb turns to Mal, but keeps talking to Ariadne...

INSERT CUT: *Cobb* WANDERS *the streets of Limbo...*

                          COBB
Searching for the right place in her mind...

INSERT CUT: *Cobb stops outside the* VICTORIAN HOUSE, MAL'S CHILD-
HOOD HOME, *looking up at it. He heads inside...*

                          COBB
And when I found that place, that secret place
where she had shut away her knowledge years
before, I broke it open...

INSERT CUT: Cobb looks around Mal's childhood bedroom. Comes to the doll's house...

> **COBB**
> I broke into the deepest recess of her mind, to give her the simplest little idea.

INSERT CUT: Cobb throws open the safe doors. Sitting on the shelf of the safe is a spinning top. On its side.

> **COBB**
> A truth that she had once known, but had chosen to forget...

INSERT CUT: Cobb picks up the totem. He SPINS it in the safe. IT SPINS AND SPINS WITHOUT END. Cobb CLOSES THE DOOR of the safe...

> **COBB**
> That her world was not real.

INSERT CUT: COBB AND MAL ARRIVE AT TRAIN TRACKS CUTTING THROUGH WASTELAND.

> **COBB (V.O.)**
> That death was a necessary escape.

They lie on the tracks looking into each other's eyes. Mal is crying. Cobb takes her hand, reassuring. He starts to speak–

> **COBB**
> *You're waiting for a train. A train that will take you far away. You know where you hope this train will take you, but you can't know for sure. Yet it doesn't matter...*

Mal looks at him across the railroad tracks. Replies–

> **MAL**
> *Because you'll be together.*

The train comes, OBLITERATING the lovers.

Back in the present– Cobb looks into Mal's eyes. She is crying.

>   COBB
>   I never thought that the idea I'd planted would
>   grow in her mind like a cancer. That even after
>   we woke...

INSERT CUT: *Cobb looks around the* HOTEL SUITE, *confused. He moves to the* CURTAINS... *Mal is on the ledge opposite.*

>   COBB
>   You'd continue to believe that your world was
>   not real...

Crying, Mal nods–

>   MAL
>   That death was the only escape?

INSERT CUT: *Mal* PLUNGES *to her death.*

>   MAL
>   You killed me.

Cobb looks at Mal. Whispers–

>   COBB
>   I was trying to save you—I'm sorry.

Mal comes in close to Cobb. Looks him over.

>   MAL
>   You infected my mind. You betrayed me. But
>   you can make amends. You can still keep your
>   promise. We can still be together... right here.
>   In our world. The world we built together.

>   CUT TO:

INT. ELEVATOR—NIGHT

Arthur hits "Play" on his music player– Edith Piaf starts to ring out, Arthur checks his detonator and we–

CUT TO:

INT. ANTECHAMBER—DAY

Eames races back in– in the relative quiet he notices MASSIVE LOW-END MUSICAL TONES. He drops his gun and goes to Fischer's side...

INT. DUCT SYSTEM, HOSPITAL COMPLEX—CONTINUOUS

Saito musters all his remaining strength as the guard emerges– Saito FIRES, dropping the guard, then COLLAPSES, the gun clattering to the duct floor... Saito is dead.

INT. ANTECHAMBER—CONTINUOUS

Eames powers up the defibrillator, puts the paddles on Fischer's chest, then POW!– he shocks him, and we–

CUT TO:

INT. PENTHOUSE (LIMBO)—DAY

LIGHTNING crackles across the sky– Ariadne sees it.

> **ARIADNE**
> We need Fischer.

> **MAL**
> You can't have him.

Cobb stares at Mal. Mesmerized.

> **COBB**
> If I stay, can she take him back?

> **ARIADNE**
> Cobb, what are you saying?

> **MAL**
> Fischer's on the porch.

> **ARIADNE**
> Cobb, you can't do this.

> **COBB**
> Go check he's alive, Ariadne.

Ariadne moves onto the porch, high above the metropolis, and we–

CUT TO:

INT. ELEVATOR—NIGHT

Arthur nods his head in time with the music, counting down, holding the detonator. He starts bracing himself, and we–

CUT TO:

INT. ANTECHAMBER—DAY

Eames recharges the defibrillator. SHOCKS Fischer again, and we–

CUT TO:

EXT. PORCH, PENTHOUSE (LIMBO)—DAY

Ariadne looks up as a LARGE BOLT OF LIGHTNING RIPS across the sky... she looks down to see Fischer, BOUND AND BLOODY, lying below the rail.

> ARIADNE
> He's here. And it's time. But you have to come with us.

Another massive lightning strike flickers across the sky–

> ARIADNE
> Cobb, I'm not going to let you lose yourself in here! You have to get back to your children!

> COBB
> Send Fischer, I have to stay—

> ARIADNE
> You can't stay here to be with her—

Cobb turns from Mal. Looks at Ariadne.

> COBB
> I'm not. Saito is dead by now. That means he's here. I have to stay here and find him.

Ariadne removes Fischer's gag– pulls him up, onto the rail. Cobb looks back at Mal.

>   COBB
>   I can't stay here to be with her because she's not
>   real.

Mal looks at Cobb, furious.

>   MAL
>   Not real? I'm the only thing you do believe in
>   anymore. Here—doesn't this feel real, Dom?

She STABS him in the chest– Cobb WHEEZES– GASPING, looking at Mal–

>   COBB
>   I wish you were. But I couldn't make you real.
>   I'm not capable of imagining you in all your
>   complexity and... perfection. As you really were.
>   You're the best I can do. And you're not real.

Mal pulls the knife and moves to STRIKE again–

>   ARIADNE
>   No!

A SHOT rings out, Mal GRABS her shoulder– Cobb turns to Ariadne, who is pointing Cobb's gun.

>   COBB
>   What're you doing?

>   ARIADNE
>   Improvising.

She KICKS Fischer off the roof– AIMS again at Mal–

Fischer DROPS as the sky LIGHTS UP WITH ELECTRICITY– Fischer SCREAMS, then GASPS, no longer falling, and we are–

INT. ANTECHAMBER—DAY

Eames pulls the defibrillator from Fischer's chest as he COUGHS AWAKE.

>   EAMES
>   Get in there—quick!

Fischer looks up at the double doors. STAGGERS to his feet. Fischer pushes open the doors to the STRONGROOM.

INT. STRONGROOM—CONTINUOUS

Fischer walks into the silent white room. At one end of the room is a bed. A figure lies in the bed. His FATHER. Breathing with tremendous difficulty. Dying. And we–

CUT TO:

EXT. PENTHOUSE (LIMBO)— DAY

Ariadne takes aim at Mal–

> COBB
> No!

Cobb holds Ariadne's gaze. She lowers the gun. And we–

CUT TO:

Eames GRABS the detonator– then moves to the door of the strong-room...

CUT TO:

INT. ELEVATOR, HOTEL—NIGHT

Arthur HITS THE DETONATOR–

INT. ELEVATOR SHAFT—CONTINUOUS

The CHARGES on the bottom of the elevator EXPLODE, and we move into EXTREME SLOW MOTION as the flames BALLOON–

CUT TO:

INT. STRONGROOM—CONTINUOUS

A RUMBLE BUILDS as Fischer approaches the bed, overcome with emotion. His Father sees him. Starts trying to speak. Fischer leans in...

> FATHER
> (hoarse whisper)
> I... was... dis... dis...

> FISCHER
>
> I know, Dad. You were disappointed that I
> couldn't be you.

The dying man SHAKES HIS HEAD with surprising energy.

> FATHER
> (whisper)
> I was disappointed... that you tried.

Fischer hears this. And we–

CUT TO:

INT. ELEVATOR SHAFT—NIGHT

The elevator car is ROCKETED along its track by the explosion–

INT. ELEVATOR—CONTINUOUS

Arthur is SMASHED against the floor of the car next to the sleepers who
SHUDDER with the force of ACCELERATION– and we–

CUT TO:

INT. ANTECHAMBER—DAY

Eames WATCHES Fischer–

> EAMES
> (to himself)
> Come on, come on...

INT. STRONGROOM—DAY

The Father collapses back onto the pillow. Fischer starts to weep. His
Father reaches out a trembling hand but when Fischer tries to hold it,
he SHAKES his son's hand away...

He is reaching for the SAFE next to his bed. His fingers fumble at the
keypad, he can't open it. His son pushes 5,2,8,4,9,1 into the keypad.
Opens it. Inside the safe is the WILL. And beside it is a HOMEMADE PIN-
WHEEL, clearly made by a child. By Fischer. He takes it out, MARVELING
at it. He turns to his father, but his father is dead.

Eames, watching from the door, HITS THE DETONATOR–

BELOW CAR
ARTHUR'S LEGS
DROP DOWN ...

SHOT
CONT'D

ARTHUR DROPS
DOWN INTO
FRAME &
SETS A CHARGE.

SHOT
CONT'D

THEN ANOTHER
ONE CLOSER
TO LENS.

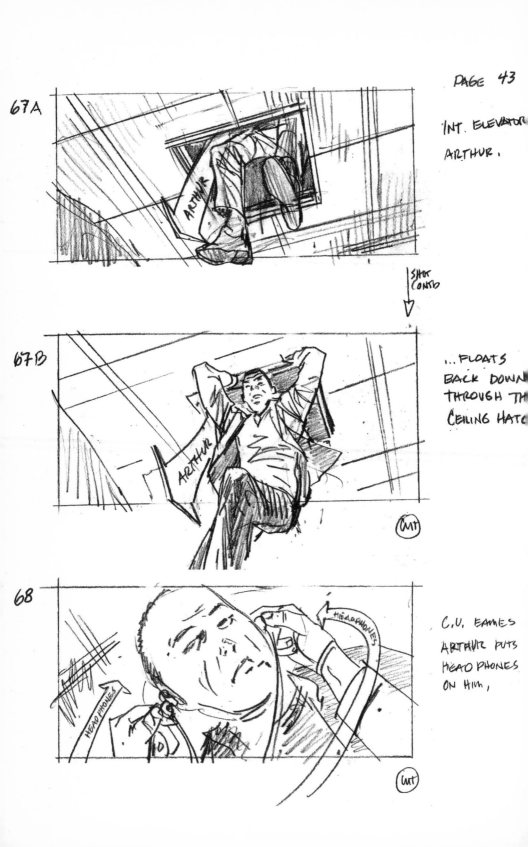

67A

PAGE 43

INT. ELEVATOR
ARTHUR.

SHOT
CONT'D

67B

...FLOATS
BACK DOWN
THROUGH TH
CEILING HATC

CUT

68

C.U. EAMES
ARTHUR PUTS
HEAD PHONES
ON HIM,

HEADPHONES

HEAD PHONES

CUT

INT. ELEVATOR
ARTHUR SECURES
HIMSELF IN THE
ELEVATOR THEN
CHECKS THE
DETONATOR

DOWN ANGLE.
THE SLEEPERS.
FLOAT

ARTHUR HITS THE
DETONATOR.

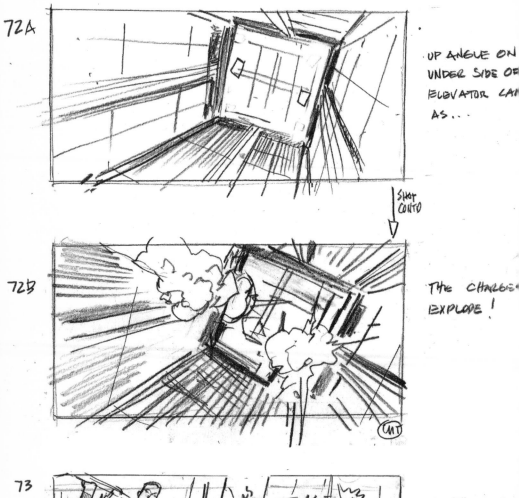

72A

UP ANGLE ON
UNDER SIDE OF
ELEVATOR CAR
AS...

SHOT
CONTD

72B

THE CHARGES
EXPLODE!

73

THE SLEEPERS
ARE PRESSED
AGAINST THE
FLOOR OF
THE ELEVATOR

A

DOWN ANGLE.
THE CAR RISES
UP TO CAMERA..

SHOT
CONT'D

B

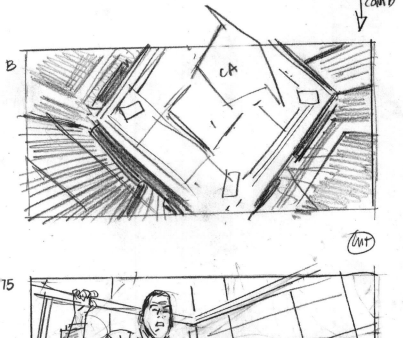

(cut)

75

(cut)

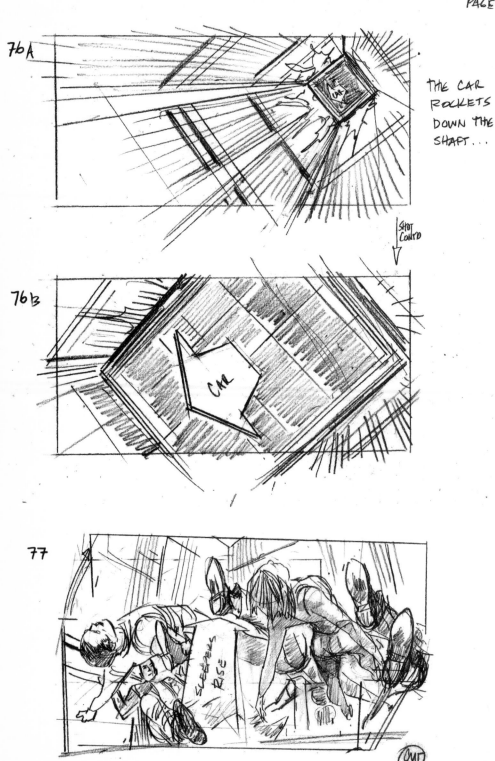

76A

THE CAR
ROCKETS
DOWN THE
SHAFT...

SHOT
CONT'D

76B

CAR

77

SLEEPERS
RISE

CUT

EXT. HOSPITAL COMPLEX—CONTINUOUS

A line of EXPLOSIONS RIPS ALONG THE LOWER WALL... the ENTIRE BUILDING STARTS TO SLIDE DOWN THE MOUNTAIN—

INT. PENTHOUSE (LIMBO)—DAY

A FIERCE WIND starts HOWLING through the house as the sky outside DARKENS. Cobb shields Mal against the blast— looks up at Ariadne, who HOLDS the railing, FIGHTING the wind—

> COBB
> That's the kick—you have to go!

> ARIADNE
> You're coming!

> COBB
> No, I'm not. I'm staying here to find Saito.
> (turns to Mal)
> And to say goodbye.

Ariadne loosens her grip on the railing...

> ARIADNE
> Don't lose yourself. Find Saito. And bring him back.

> COBB
> I will.

Ariadne lets the wind pull her off the edge— FALLING— and we—

INT. ANTECHAMBER—CONTINUOUS

Ariadne DROPS as the FLOOR COLLAPSES— her eyes SNAP OPEN—

EXT. PENTHOUSE (LIMBO)—DAY

Cobb holds Mal in his arms. The wind DIES...

> MAL
> We'd be together forever. You promised me.

> COBB
> I know. But we can't. And I'm sorry.

> MAL
>
> You remember when you asked me to marry you? You said you dreamt that we'd grow old together.

> COBB
>
> And we did...

Mal looks at Cobb... thinking. Remembering.

INSERT CUT: TWO ELDERLY PEOPLE (MAL AND COBB) WALK THROUGH LIMBO... ACROSS A WASTELAND... TWO ELDERLY HANDS CLUTCH EACH OTHER AS THEY LIE DOWN ON THE RAILROAD TRACK...

> COBB
>
> I miss you more than I can bear... but we had our time together. And now I have to let go...

She nods, weakly. Cobb holds Mal as her eyes close... DYING... and we–

INT. STRONGROOM—CONTINUOUS

Fischer and his Father's body DROP AWAY–

INT. ELEVATOR—NIGHT

Ariadne DROPS inside the ROCKETING ELEVATOR, and as it SMASHES INTO THE TOP OF THE SHAFT Ariadne SMASHES INTO–

INT./EXT. VAN INTO RIVER—DAY

THE WATER, THE VAN CRUNCHING WITH THE IMPACT– WATER CRASH-ING THROUGH THE BROKEN WINDOWS FLOODING THE INTERIOR...

Fischer's EYES OPEN, PANICKING– he UNBUCKLES HIMSELF, pushes out of the broken window– STOPS, goes back to UNBUCKLE Browning and DRAG him out–

EXT. RIVER—CONTINUOUS

Fischer breaks the surface with Browning, who COUGHS and GASPS. He starts PULLING for the near bank, struggling through the rain-impacted water–

INT. VAN, UNDERWATER—CONTINUOUS

Ariadne, Arthur and Yusuf wait calmly underwater. They are sharing TWO REGULATORS pulled from beneath the front seat. Arthur turns to Saito. There is blood in the water around Saito's belly– his eyes are LIFELESS– Arthur feels for a pulse... turns to Cobb, whose eyes are lifeless... Ariadne GRABS Arthur's elbow, pulling him away...

EXT. RIVERBANK—MOMENTS LATER

Fischer turns Browning/Eames over. They lie there, exhausted.

> BROWNING
> I'm sorry, Robert.

Fischer stares at the rain on the water.

> FISCHER
> The will means that Dad wanted me to be my
> own man, not live for him.
> > (turns to Browning)
> And I'm going to, Uncle Peter.

Browning nods. Wipes the rain from his face. In the puddle beside them, the reflection is not Browning, but Eames.

EXT. UNDERNEATH BRIDGE IN THE RAIN—MOMENTS LATER

Arthur sits on the riverbank, breathing heavily.

> ARTHUR
> What happened?

> ARIADNE
> Cobb stayed.

> ARTHUR
> With Mal?

> ARIADNE
> No. To find Saito.

Arthur looks out at the water below the bridge.

> ARTHUR
> He'll be lost...

                              ARIADNE
                No. He'll be alright.

        And we–

                                                            CUT TO:

EXT. DAWN. CRASHING SURF.

        The waves TOSS a BEARDED MAN onto wet sand.

        As the Japanese Security Guard turns him onto his back, we realize
        that this is Cobb– OLDER. WEARY. TRAVELLED...

INT. DINING ROOM, CASTLE—DAY

        Cobb WOLFS his food. The Elderly Japanese Man (Saito, 90 years old)
        watches him.

                              SAITO
                So... have you come to kill me?

        Cobb does not look up.

                              SAITO
                I've been waiting for someone to come for me...

                              COBB
                Someone from your half-remembered dream...?

        Saito peers at Cobb.

                              SAITO
                Cobb? Not possible—he and I were young men
                together. And I am an old man...

                              COBB
                Filled with regret?

        Saito REMEMBERS, nods...

                              SAITO
                Waiting to die alone, yes.

        Cobb is STARING at something on the table.

> COBB
>
> I came back for you... I came to remind you of
> what you once knew...

Cobb gestures at the table. Saito follows his gaze down to the polished
surface of the table...

> COBB
>
> That this world is not real.

The top is STILL SPINNING PERFECTLY, AS IF IT WILL NEVER TOPPLE.
Saito looks at the top. Then back to Cobb.

> SAITO
>
> You came to convince me to honor our arrange-
> ment?

> COBB
>
> Yes. And to take a leap of faith.

As Saito-san listens to Cobb, he looks at the GUN on the table between
them...

> COBB
>
> Come back and we'll be young men together
> again.

The elderly Saito looks at Cobb. Nods. And we–

CUT TO:

INT. FIRST CLASS CABIN, 747—DAY

Ariadne watches Cobb. His eyes are closed.

> FLIGHT ATTENDANT (O.S.)
>
> Hot towel, sir?

His EYES FLICKER OPEN. He takes the towel with a nod. Ariadne smiles.
Relieved.

> FLIGHT ATTENDANT
>
> We'll be landing in Los Angeles in about twenty
> minutes. Do you need immigration forms?

Cobb nods. Takes a landing card. Looks around the cabin.

Saito is WATCHING him. Serious. Haunted. Holding Cobb's gaze, SAITO PICKS UP THE PHONE AND DIALS. Cobb nods thanks...

INT. ARRIVALS, LAX—LATER

Cobb steps forwards to the IMMIGRATION OFFICIAL. Hands him his passport. Nervous. The Official takes a beat, looks Cobb up and down, then WHUMP!– the passport is stamped. As Cobb takes it back, he spots Ariadne at the next counter. She nods at him. He nods back. Then moves off...

As Cobb passes through baggage claim, he exchanges subtle greetings with Eames and Yusuf.

Arthur smiles broadly at Cobb. Cobb brushes past Fischer, who glances back at him as if thinking maybe he should know him, then moves on...

As Cobb emerges into the crowded arrivals hall, he spots Professor Miles, waving at him...

INT. KITCHEN, COBB AND MAL'S HOUSE—DAY

Cobb enters with Miles. Drops his bags. Moves to the table, looking out at the overgrown garden. He reaches into his pocket, takes out his pewter spinning top, lowers it to the table and SPINS IT– a CHILD'S SHOUT makes him look up–

Through the window, James and Philippa have run into view, playing, THEIR FACES TURNED AWAY... Cobb STARES at the back of his children's heads... Miles moves to the window and KNOCKS on the glass–

James and Philippa TURN– see their Dad. He steps to the window, watching their BRIGHT FACES SHINING as they run towards him...

Behind him, on the table, the spinning top is STILL SPINNING. And we–

FADE OUT.

CREDITS.

END.

APPENDICES

Portable Automated Somnacin IntraVenous (PASIV) Device
Instruction Manual MV-235A

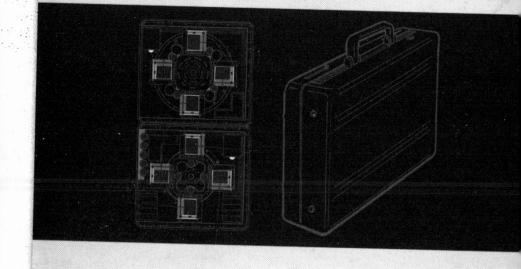

Doc: 2233356-88 A-19

① INTRODUCTION

The Portable Automated Somnacin IntraVenous (PASIV) Device provides precise control and stabilization for Somnacin dosage and delivery in the field.

See Figure 1a and 1b

- Configurable control settings for the accurate monitoring and adjustment of Somnacin dosage levels.

- 12' IV lines for versatile in the field set-up.

- LED display with atomized timer for monitoring precise flow rates.

- Synchronization monitoring chip for flow check monitoring and automated adjustment to optimize output flow.

- Lithium iodide batteries with life of 200 hours.

- Additional vial storage for multiple doses in the field.

- Case lock for prevention of system tampering.

- Memory backup for retention of infusion output data.

- Easy access to fuses and batteries for replacement.

Figure 1a

Figure 1b

2 PHYSICAL DESCRIPTION

2a • PASIV DEVICE

A Case Lock – For maximum security.

B Synchronized Injection Piston – Gas-tight reciprocating pump accurately measures Somnacin from its vial and dispels via IV infusion line.

C Vial Store – Four reinforced storage compartments for additional standard Somnacin vials.

D LED Timer Display – Timer duration accurate to 1/100th of a second.

E Manual Valve – For use in the event of a power interruption.

F IV Infusion Line – 18 gauge non-PVC flexible plastic tubing.

G IV Output Coupling – Brass coupling allowing uninterrupted IV infusion line runs while case is closed and locked.

H IV Cannula – Pre-attached cannula with retractable needles.

I Retainer Plate – Made of non-conductive titanium alloy.

J Fuse – The fuse compartment can be accessed with a Phillips-head screwdriver.

K Compression Flange – The custom mold maintains an airtight seal.

L Injection Activation Trigger – Enables Somnacin infusion.

M Synchronization Monitoring Chip – The chip monitors and automatically adjusts flow output at registered levels. Monitoring chips can be removed and attuned off-unit.

N Vial Cradle – Secures Somnacin to retainer and IV trigger.

O Retractable Spool – This compression spring coil collects and releases the IV cable.

P Battery Pack – Houses custom lithium iodide batteries.

Q Carrying Handle – Made of a nanocomposite polymer.

③ PRECAUTIONS

3a • PRECAUTIONS

- A trained engineer familiar with the PASIV device should verify settings before use.

- Use only IV infusion lines with the PASIV designation.

- Although the PASIV injection engine is a self-filtering and cleaning device, replace IV infusion lines regularly.

- The PASIV device should be used with the supervision of either a trained engineer or other qualified professional.

- Diagnostics should be run on the PASIV device every month or more frequently with increased use.

The PASIV device is designed solely for the dosage and administration of Somnacin and should not be used for Somnacin derivatives or generics or any other intravenous infusions or transfusions as this could result in serious injury or death.

(4) OPERATION

4a • PRIMING THE PUMP

1. Place your PASIV device on a flat, sturdy surface, free of clutter, dust, or other contaminants.

Disclaimer: It is recommended that individuals handling the PASIV device should clean and sanitize their hands immediately before usage to reduce maintenance and upkeep on the device, as well as for sanitary purposes during the injection and infusion process.

2. Unlock the device by depressing the case lock button on the front left of the case.

NOTE: If your case does not unlock, please contact your PASIV device support staff team member agent during designated call times.

3. Open the case by simultaneously depressing the two latches on either side of the carrying handle.

See Figure 4a-1

Caution: The lid is partially spring-loaded and will open several inches after unlatching.

4. Carefully but firmly insert Somnacin vials into cradles. When the Somnacin vial is firmly in place there will be a soft click and the corresponding LED display will illuminate.

Note: It is possible to insert vials of Somnacin into the reserve vial store in the upper left of the compartment at any time.

See Figure 4a-2

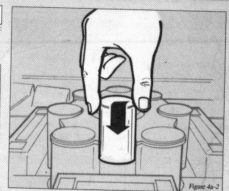

Figure 4a-2

5. Adjust the dosage level by pressing either of the two white buttons on either side of the LED display. Dosages are automatically converted from flow rate (mL/hr) to practical time.

See Figure 4a-3

(A) The button to the right of the LED display will increase the dosage; the button to the left of the LED display will decrease the dosage. These buttons will be non-functioning once the device is activated.

(B) Hint: Pressing and holding either of these buttons will steadily increase the rate of dosage amounts.

Figure 4a-1

Figure 4a-3

4 OPERATION

4a • PRIMING THE PUMP

6. Lock dosage levels by pressing both white buttons simultaneously.

A The LED screen should flash "LOCKED" and a small hiss should be heard as the injection piston engages. The screen will then intermittently display the word "LOCKED" with the dosage amount.

B To unlock a cradle, press and hold both white buttons simultaneously until the LED screen reads "UNLOCKED" and the injection piston disengages. You can now adjust dosage levels.

NOTE: IV infusion lines will not uncoil from their retractable spool if the corresponding cradle is not locked.

7. Repeat steps 4 through 6 until all cradles are full or you have inserted as many vials as you need.

8. Once all cradles are locked, close and lock the case until you are ready to prep your participants for infusion.

④ OPERATION

4b • PREPPING FOR INFUSION

1. Participants should be in a comfortable reclined position for infusion, free from excessive light or noise, as these elements may be disruptive.
   - Ⓐ Light-blocking masks and noise-dampening headsets may be employed.
   - Ⓑ Prepare a similar space for yourself, as operator.

> **Disclaimer:** It is recommended that individuals handling the PASIV device during the injection and infusion process should clean and sanitize their hands, as well as keep a biohazard disposal container for needles and cannula used in the injection process.

2. Place the PASIV device approximately in the middle or center of your participants on a stable, sturdy surface.

   NOTE: If your case is already open, skip ahead to step 5.

   See Figure 4b-1

3. Unlock the device by depressing the case lock button on the front left of the case.

4. Open the case by simultaneously depressing the two latches on either side of the carrying handle.

5. Remove the cap from one of the IV output couplings.

   See Figure 4b-2

6. Gently pull the corresponding IV infusion line from its retractable spool and feed through the coupling.

   See Figure 4b-3

7. Swab the wrist of the participant with an alcohol pad or disinfectant solution.

8. Squeeze the cannula at the end of the IV line to expose the two injection needles.

   See Figure 4b-4

9. Insert injection needles into the wrist of the participant.

   See Figure 4b-5

10. Repeat steps 5-9 for any participants and finally, for yourself.

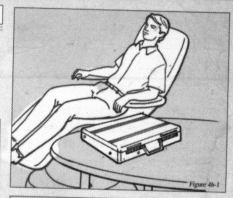

Figure 4b-1

Figure 4b-2

Figure 4b-3

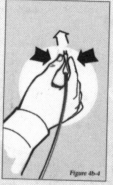

Figure 4b-4

Figure 4b-5

4 OPERATION

4c • INITIATING INFUSION

1. Double-check that all participants have their IV lines firmly attached.

2. Press the injection activation trigger. *See Figure 4c-1*

3. Check to see that the LED timer displays for all participants are counting down.

4. Move swiftly but carefully to your resting place and recline.

4 OPERATION

4d • POWERING DOWN

1. Check all LED monitors to make sure Somnacin flow has ceased.

2. Dip a cotton ball (or similar) in alcohol or disinfectant.

3. Remove the cannula from the participant, pressing the cotton ball against the skin.

4. Holding the end of the IV line in one hand, gently tug the IV line three inches from the spool. The spool is retractable and should firmly and smoothly pull the IV line back onto the spool. *See Figure 4d-1*

🅐 Hint: Guide the IV line onto the spool to form a less bulky coil.

5. Instruct the participant to hold for thirty seconds or until bleeding stops.

6. Repeat steps 2-6 for all participants.

7. Close and lock lid. The device will power down naturally.

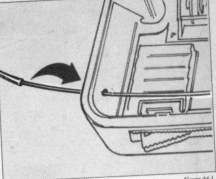

Figure 4d-1

LEONARDO DiCAPRIO KEN WATANABE JOSEPH GORDON-LEVITT MARION COTILLARD ELLEN PAGE TOM HARDY CILLIAN MURPHY TOM BERENGER and MICHAEL CAINE

YOUR MIND IS THE SCENE OF THE CRIME.

INCEPTION

FROM THE DIRECTOR OF **THE DARK KNIGHT**

LEGENDARY PICTURES

WARNER BROS. PICTURES

FILM CREDITS

WARNER BROS. PICTURES
©2010 Warner Bros. Ent. All Rights Reserved

LEGENDARY
P I C T U R E S

"INCEPTION"

Written and Directed by
CHRISTOPHER NOLAN
Produced by
EMMA THOMAS
Produced by
CHRISTOPHER NOLAN
Executive Producers
CHRIS BRIGHAM
THOMAS TULL
Director of Photography
WALLY PFISTER, A.S.C.
Production Designer
GUY HENDRIX DYAS
Edited by
LEE SMITH, A.C.E.
Co-Producer
JORDAN GOLDBERG
Music by
HANS ZIMMER
Costumes Designed by
JEFFREY KURLAND
Special Effects Supervisor
CHRIS CORBOULD
Visual Effects Supervisor
PAUL FRANKLIN
Casting by
JOHN PAPSIDERA, CSA

LEONARDO DICAPRIO

"INCEPTION"

KEN WATANABE
JOSEPH GORDON-LEVITT
MARION COTILLARD
ELLEN PAGE
TOM HARDY
CILLIAN MURPHY
TOM BERENGER
and MICHAEL CAINE
DILEEP RAO
LUKAS HAAS
TALULAH RILEY
A WARNER BROS. PICTURES Presentation
In Association with LEGENDARY PICTURES
A SYNCOPY Production
A Film by CHRISTOPHER NOLAN

Unit Production Manager	JAN FOSTER
First Assistant Director	NILO OTERO
Second Assistant Director	BRANDON LAMBDIN

Cobb	LEONARDO DICAPRIO
Arthur	JOSEPH GORDON-LEVITT
Ariadne	ELLEN PAGE
Eames	TOM HARDY
Saito	KEN WATANABE
Yusuf	DILEEP RAO
Robert Fischer, Jr.	CILLIAN MURPHY
Browning	TOM BERENGER
Mal	MARION COTILLARD
Maurice Fischer	PETE POSTLETHWAITE
Miles	MICHAEL CAINE
Nash	LUKAS HAAS
Tadashi	TAI-LI LEE
Phillipa (3 years)	CLAIRE GEARE
James (20 months)	MAGNUS NOLAN
Phillipa (5 years)	TAYLOR GEARE
James (3 years)	JOHNATHAN GEARE
Japanese Security Guard	TOHORU MASAMUNE
Saito's Attendant	YUJI OKUMOTO
Elderly Bald Man	EARL CAMERON
Lawyer	RYAN HAYWARD
Flight Attendant	MIRANDA NOLAN
Cab Driver	RUSS FEGA
Thin Man	TIM KELLEHER
Blonde	TALULAH RILEY
Bridge Sub Cons	NICOLAS CLERC
	CORALIE DEDYKERE
	SILVIE LAGUNA
	VIRGILE BRAMLY
	JEAN-MICHEL DAGORY

Penrose Sub Cons	HELENA CULLINAN
	MARK FLEISCHMANN
	SHELLEY LANG
Bar Sub Cons	ADAM COLE
	JACK MURRAY
	KRAIG THORNBER
	ANGELA NATHENSON
	NATASHA BEAUMONT
Lobby Sub Cons	MARC RADUCCI
	CARL GILLIARD
	JILL MADDRELL
	ALEX LOMBARD
	NICOLE PULLIAM
Fischer's Jet Captain	PETER BASHAM
Immigration Officer	MICHAEL GASTON
Businessmen	FELIX SCOTT
	ANDREW PLEAVIN
Private Nurse	LISA REYNOLDS
Fischer's Driver	JASON TENDELL
Old Cobb	JACK GILROY
Old Mal	SHANNON WELLES
Stunt Coordinators	TOM STRUTHERS
	SY HOLLANDS
	BRENT WOOLSEY
Stunts	DANNY LE BOYER
	ANDY BRADSHAW
	RICHARD L. BUCHER
	RICHARD BURDEN
	ALLISON CAETANO
	BRUCE CAIN
	TOM COHAN
	ELIZA COLEMAN
	GEORGE COTTLE
	STEVE DeCASTRO
	JAKE DEWITT
	WADE EASTWOOD
	RICK ENGLISH
	ROEL FAILMA
	MARK FICHERA
	MARIE FINK
	STEVE GRIFFIN
	BOBBY HANLON
	ADAM HART
	LOGAN HOLLADAY
	GARY HOPTROUGH
	JASON HUNJAN
	STEPHEN IZZI
	TERRY JACKSON
	RUTH JENKINS
	LUKE KEARNEY
	JESS KING
	MAURICE LEE
	TERRY J. LEONARD
	JAMES LEW
	MICHAEL LI
	NITO LARIOZA
	DIANA R. LUPO
	RICK MILLER
	STEVE OEDING
	MONTE PERLIN
	NORBERT PHILLIPS
	ANDY PILGRIM
	MARK RAYNER
	REX J. REDDICK
	SIMON RHEE
	TRACEY RUGGIERO

BRANDON SEBEK
DIZ SHARPE
GUNTHER SIMON
PAUL SKLAR
MARVIN STEWART-CAMPBELL
JOHN STREET
MELISSA R. STUBBS
MENS-SANA TAMAKLOE
PHILIP TAN
MARLOW WARRINGTON-MATTEI
CHRISSY WEATHERSBY
JIM WILKEY
HARRY WOWCHUK
RICHARD WU
RYAN YOUNG

Additional Editor	JOHN LEE
Post Production Supervisor	DAVID E. HALL
Visual Effects Producer	MIKE CHAMBERS
Sound Designer/Supervising Sound Editor	RICHARD KING
Re-Recording Mixers	LORA HIRSCHBERG
	GARY A. RIZZO
Production Sound Mixer	ED NOVICK
Production Controller	HELEN MEDRANO
Script Supervisor	STEVEN ROGER GEHRKE
Supervising Art Director	BRAD RICKER
Art Directors	LUKE FREEBORN
	DEAN WOLCOTT
Assistant Art Director	JOSH LUSBY
Set Decorators	LARRY DIAS
	DOUG MOWAT
Art Department Coordinator	CHARLOTTE RAYBOURN
Leadman	SCOTT BOBBITT
On Set Dresser	ERIC ROOD
Graphic Designer	WILLIAM ELISCU
Set Designers	MARK HITCHLER
	GREG HOOPER
	LARRY HUBBS
	BOB FECHTMAN
	SAM PAGE
Storyboard Artist	GABRIEL HARDMAN
Lead Model Maker	JASON MAHAKIAN
Buyers	SARA GARDNER-GAIL
	AMANDA MOSS SERINO
Art Researcher	DOMINIQUE ARCADIO
Art Archivist	CALE WILBANKS
First Assistant Camera	BOB HALL
Second Assistant Camera	DANIEL MCFADDEN
Additional Second Assistant Camera	DAN SCHROER
Loader	BEN PERRY
Underwater Director of Photography	PETE ROMANO
Ultimate Arm Technicians	DEAN BAILEY
	LEV YEVSTRATOV
Aerial Director of Photography	HANS BJERNO
Helicopter Pilot	CRAIG HOSKING
Still Photographers	MELISSA MOSELEY
	STEVE VAUGHAN
Boom Operator	BRIAN ROBINSON
Sound Utility	STERLING MOORE
Key Video Assist / Computer Video Supervisor	KEVIN BOYD
Production Supervisor	ELONA TSOU
Production Office Coordinator	SARAH SPEARING
Asst. Production Office Coordinator	BRYAN DAVIS
Production Secretary	MORGAN AHLBORN
Travel Coordinator	CARRIE OYER
Production Accountants	CARLO PRATTO

	ANTHEA "ANTS" STRANGIS
Location Accountants	FREDERIC GREENE
	BOBBIE JOHNSON
First Assistant Accountant	PAM DES VIGNE
Costume Supervisor	BOB MORGAN
Assistant Costume Designer	TERRY ANDERSON
Key Costumers	SONNY MERRITT
	KENDALL ERRAIR
Mr. DiCaprio's Costumer	COOKIE LOPEZ-FAHEY
Set Costumers	KELLY PORTER
	ELIZABETH FRANK
Costumers	JACK TAGGART
	IVORY STANTON
	KURT J. BLACKWELL
	PABLO BORGES
	NINA PADOVANO
Hair Department Head	JAN ALEXANDER
Key Hairstylist	TERRY BALIEL
Mr. DiCaprio's Hairstylist	KATHRYN L. BLONDELL
Make-up Department Head	LUISA ABEL
Key Make-up Artist	JAY WEJEBE
Make-up Artist	MAGGIE E. ELLIOTT
Mr. DiCaprio's Make-up Artist	SIAN GRIGG
Chief Lighting Technician	CORY GERYAK
Assistant Chief Lighting Technician	LARRY SUSHINSKI
Rigging Gaffer	CHARLES H. MCINTYRE
Key Grip	RAY GARCIA
Best Boy Grip	ROD FARLEY
Dolly Grip	DAVE PEARLBERG
Rigging Key Grip	BLAKE PIKE
Special Effects Coordinator	SCOTT FISHER
Senior Special Effects Technicians	ANDY SMITH
	MARIO VANILLO
Special Effects Technicians	JOHN J. DOWNEY
	JIM ROLLINS
	LEO SOLIS
Second Second Assistant Director	GREG PAWLIK
Additional Second Assistant Director	LAUREN PASTERNACK
Assistant to Mr. Nolan	STACEY KELLY
Assistant to Ms. Thomas	DEREK THORN
Assistant to Mr. Brigham	AYA TANIMURA
Assistant to Mr. DiCaprio	JASON IRIZARRY
Assistant to Ms. Page	CARRIE GOOCH
Assistant to Mr. Watanabe	SATCH WATANABE
Office Staff Assistants	TONY FANG
	MARK MCSORLEY
	ALEXANDRA PURSGLOVE
	ALEX WESTMORE
	ANDREW WILL
	HELLEN MARIN
	KRISTEN MASON
Location Managers	ILT JONES
	JJ HOOK
Key Assistant Location Managers	MANDI DILLIN
	KAI EPHRON
	RONALD HAYNES
	MANNY PADILLA
	DAVID PARK
	ALFONSO RUIZ
	MICHAEL WESLEY
	NANCY WONG
Assistant Location Manager	KEOMANEE VILAYTHONG
Property Master	SCOTT MAGINNIS

Assistant Property Masters	GLENN FORBES
	ERICK GARIBAY
Armorer	HARRY LU
Construction Coordinator	C. JONAS KIRK
Modeler Gang Boss Moldshop Supervisor	DAVID COHEN
Paint Supervisor	FRANK PIERCY
Greens Foreman	C. LILOA WONG
Standby Painter	CARMINE GUGLIA
Picture Car Coordinator	TYLER GAISFORD
Transportation Coordinator	DENNY CAIRA
Transportation Captain	MIKE SHANNON
Craft Service	LEAH AMIR
Medics	JASON INMAN
	GENE STARZENSKI
Catering	CHEF ROBERT CATERING
Key Set Assistant	ZACK L. SMITH
Set Production Assistants	SAM ALVELO
	JEFF HUBBARD
	OLIVIA "MOUSY" MCCALLUM
	CRYSTAL MUNSON
	MANDY NOACK
	GERSON PAZ
	ADAM SLUTSKY
	AMY VENGHAUS
	RYAN YOUNG
	POLLY MORGAN
	LEIGHTON BOWERS
	LUIS RODRIGUEZ
	JAYSON CHANG
Casting Associate	JENNIFER CRAM
Casting Assistant	DYLAN JURY
Extras Casting	MARYELLEN AVIANO
Dialect Coach	FRANCIE BROWN
Unit Publicist	AMANDA BRAND
First Assistant Editors	ERIC LEWY
	LAURA RINDNER
Assistant Editors	DONALD LIKOVICH
	CHRISTY RICHMOND
	PAULA SUHY
	ALEXIS SEYMOUR
	KATIE HEDRICH
Post Production Accountant	NOLAN MEDRANO
Post Production Coordinator	HAILEY MURRAY
Post Production Assistants	CHRIS GOBLE
	BOBBIE SHAY
	JEFF WINKLE
First Assistant Sound Editors	ANDREW BOCK
	LINDA YEANEY
ADR Editor	R. J. KIZER
Dialogue Editor	HUGO WENG
Sound Effects Editors	MICHAEL W. MITCHELL
	PAUL BEROLZHEIMER
	BRYAN WATKINS
Foley Supervisor	CHRISTOPHER FLICK
Foley Editor	BRUCE TANIS
Foley Artists	JOHN ROESCH
	ALYSON DEE MOORE
Foley Mixer	MARY JO LANG
ADR Mixer	THOMAS J. O'CONNELL
Sound Effects Recording Mixers	JOHN PAUL FASAL
	ERIC POTTER
Additional Re-Recording Mixer	MICHAEL BABCOCK
Re-Recordist	ERIC FLICKINGER
Supervising Music Editor	ALEX GIBSON
Music Editor	RYAN RUBIN
Assistant Music Editors	PETER OSO SNELL

	MIKE HIGHAM
Score Produced and Additional Music by	LORNE BALFE
Ambient Music Design	MEL WESSON
Synth Programming	HANS ZIMMER
	HOWARD SCARR
Guitar	JOHNNY MARR
Orchestrator	BRUCE L. FOWLER
Orchestra Conducted by	MATT DUNKLEY
Digital Instrument Design	MARK WHERRY
Music Production Services	STEVEN KOFSKY
Music Score Consultant	GAVIN GREENAWAY
Score Coordinator	ANDREW ZACK
Score Recorded by	GEOFF FOSTER
Score Mixed by	ALAN MEYERSON
Visual Effects Production Supervisor	MONETTE DUBIN
Visual Effects Editor	STEVE MILLER
Visual Effects Director of Photography	MARK WEINGARTNER
Visual Effects Camera	WAYNE BAKER
Visual Effects On Set Data Wrangler	JOE WEHMEYER
Visual Effects Assistant Editors	SCOTT WESLEY ROSS
	STEVE RHEE
Visual Effects Assistant Coordinators	KATIE STETSON
	RICHARD WILSON
	DOUG NICHOLAS
Visual Effects Production Assistants	KIERAN AHERN
	MATTHEW EBERLE
	SHUN TSUCHIYA
	CURTIS MICHAEL DAVEY
Titles by	PJF PRODUCTIONS, INC.
Negative Cutter	MARY BETH SMITH
Color Timer	DAVID ORR

UNITED KINGDOM

Unit Production Manager	MARK MOSTYN
Production Coordinator	KATHERINE TIBBETTS
Assistant Production Coordinators	HALLAM RICE EDWARDS
	TOM FORBES
Location Accountant	CHRISTIAN FELDHAUS
First Assistant Accountant	BECKY MAXWELL
Supervising Art Director	FRANK WALSH
Art Directors	JASON KNOX JOHNSTON
	PAUL LAUGIER
	ANDY THOMSON
Art Department Coordinator	JENNIFER LEWICKI
Supervising Aerial Coordinator	MIKE WOODLEY
Assistant Editor	BEN RENTON
Post Production Assistant	KATE DENNING
Second Assistant Directors	RICHARD GRAYSMARK
	PAULA TURNBULL
Third Assistant Directors	SARAH HOOD
	JAMES RAINER
B Camera Operator/Steadicam	GRAHAM HALL
UK Casting	SYSON GRAINGER
Catering	VINCE JORDAN
Construction Coordinator	MALCOLM ROBERTS
Costume Supervisor	KENNY CROUCH
Gaffer	ANDY LONG
Rigging Gaffer	IAN FRANKLIN
Key Grip	RYAN MONRO
Location Manager	NICK DAUBENY
Property Master	BARRY GIBBS
Picture Car Coordinator	IAN CLARKE
Set Decorator	LISA CHUGG
Special Effects Floor Supervisor	PETER NOTLEY

Special Effects Workshop Supervisors	KEVIN HERD
	PAUL KNOWLES
	TOM MURTAGH
	ROY QUINN
Transportation Captain	STEVE BRIGDEN
Video Operator/Coordinator	STEPHEN LEE

CANADA

Associate Producer	THOMAS HAYSLIP
Unit Production Manager	BRIAN LESLIE PARKER
Production Coordinator	KIM GODDARD-RAINS
First Assistant Accountant	BARBARA UNRAU
Art Director	BILL IVES
Construction Coordinator	ALF ARNDT
Set Decorator	PAUL HEALY
Ski Camera Director of Photography	CHRIS PATTERSON
Best Boy Grip	CHARLES EHRLINGER
Dolly Grip	MARK WOJCIECHOWSKI
Location Manager	RINO PACE
Assistant Location Manager	JAY ST. LOUIS
Transportation Coordinator	COLEMAN ROBINSON
Special Effects Coordinator	JASON PARADIS

Production Services (France)	PENINSULA FILM
Line Producer (France)	JOHN BERNARD
Production Manager (France)	GILLES CASTERA
Location Manager (France)	ARNAUD KAISER
Production Services (Morocco)	ZAK PRODUCTIONS
Line Producer (Morocco)	ZAK ALAOUI
Production Manager (Morocco)	SAM BRECKMAN
Location Manager (Morocco)	EMMA PILL
Production Supervisor (Japan)	MITCHELL DAUTERIVE
Media Wave Inc. Producer (Japan)	YOSHIKUNI TAKI
Cross Media, Inc. Producer (Japan)	KANJIRO SAKURA
Unit Production Manager (Japan)	SHUHEI OKABAYASHI

Visual Effects by DOUBLE NEGATIVE LTD
Visual Effects Supervisors

Andrew Lockley	Peter Bebb	Rob Hodgson

Visual Effects Producer
Matt Plummer

Visual Effects Associate Producers
Nina Fallon   Natalie Stopford

Visual Effects Coordinators

Katy Mummery	Michelle Kuginis	Peter Olliff
Arabella Gilbert	Ali Ingham	

CG Supervisors

Phillip Johnson	Aleks Pejic	Dan Neal
Philippe LePrince	Stuart Farley	Alison Wortman
Vanessa Boyce		

CG Lighting Supervisor
Bruno Baron

Lead CG Lighting Artists

Maxx Leong	James Benson	Clement Gerard
Alexandre Millet		

CG Lighting Artists

Peter Ocampo	Cenay Oekman	Ellen Poon
Stephen Borneman	Paul Burton	Huw Evans
Paul Brannan	John Seru	Jacob Slutsky
Mark Masson	Alistair Darby	James Guy
Lee Tibbetts	Paul McWilliams	Clare Williams
Becky Graham	Arild Anfinnsen	Stephen Ellis
Thomas Carrick	Brian Silva	Paul Ducker

CG Modellers

Azzard Gordon	Eugene Lipkin	Carlos Poon
Henrik Soder	Mikael Brosset	Marko Schobel
Will Correia		

Texture Artists

Patsy Yuen	Keziah Bailey	Mike Bain

CG Effects Supervisor
Nicola Hoyle

Lead CG Effects Artists

Kai Stavginski	May Leung	Luca Zappala
Danielle Brooks	David Hyde	Chris Ung
Jeremy Smith		

CG Effects Artists

Jean Claude Nouchy	Joe Thornley	Muhittin Bilginer
Heiko Sulberg	Sotiris Georghiou	Dominic Carus
Paul Boyd	Terry Marriott	Erik Tvedt

Animators
Dorian Knapp   Stewart Ash

Matchmove Supervisor
Daniel Baldwin

Matchmove Artists

Richard Burnside	Ryan Woodward	David Goubitz
Jay Fleming	Andy Potter	Rob Seaton
Fanny Roche	Julien Fourvel	Michael Lyle
James Mulholland	Timothy Russell	Jonathan Perez
Sam Hanover	Andrew Macleod	Matt Sadler
Laurence Priest	Sophie Robinson	Sean Whelan
Joe Dennis	Michael Cashmore	Ross Wilkinson

Compositing Sequence Supervisors

Graham Page	George Zwier	Astrid Busser-Casas
Tilman Paulin	Jan Maroske	Richard R. Reed
Scott Pritchard	Tom Hocking	Sean Heuston
	Julian Gnass	

Compositors

Paul Scott	Susanne Becker	Per Mork-Jensen
Scott Marriot	Sonny Pye	Adam Hammond
Tom Middleton	Ami Patel	Miodrag Colombo
Jamie McPherson	Mark Payne	Bimla Chall
Joerg Baier	Kim Wiseman	Daniel Rauchwerger
Romain Bouvard	Annie Nakamura	Ben Taylor
Debbi Coleman	Kirsty Clark	John Galloway
Charlie Noble	Tom Luff	Jeremy Hey
Matthew Jacques	Graham Day	Ben Hicks
Alice Mitchell	Carlo Scaduto	Bronwyn Edwards
Peter Vickery	Helgi Laxdal	Andi Dorfan
Ciaran Crowley	Giuseppe Tagliavini	Nik Brownlee
Oscar Tornincasa	Sharon Warmington	Richard Bain
Helen Wood		

Rotoscope Artists

Yoav Dolev	Luke Bigley	Kevin Norris
Ellen Miki	Philip Smith	Yousaf Main
Christopher Jaques	Sam Dawes	Enrik Pavdeja
Jean-Francois Leroux	Ben Dick	Edward Andrews
Renaud Madeline	Daniel Leatherdale	Ana Gomes
Charlie Ellis	Luke Ballard	Dan Churchill
Yuko Kimoto	Mary Stroumpouli	Kamelia Chabane
Wesley Roberts	Tara Roseblade	Vincent Chang
Lester Brown	Stephen Tew	

Visual Effects Art Director
Gurel Mehmet

Matte Painters

Dimitri Delecovias	Diccon Alexander
Simon Gustafsson	Philippe Gaulier
Visual Effects Editor	Leanne Young

Assistant Visual Effects Editors
Josh Lawson   Claudia Maharaj

Software Development

Laurent Hamery	Oliver Harding	Dane Barney
Davide Vercelli	Will Harrower	Jennifer Wood
Peter Kyme	David Minor	Paul Hogbin
Ian Masters	Jeff Clifford	Jonathan Stroud
James Roberts	Marie Tollec	Matthias Scharfenberg
Oliver James	Siobhan Platten	Ted Waine
Dan Bailey	Luke Goddard	Trina Roy

Technical Support

Peter Hanson	Miles Drake	Simon Speight

Visual Effects by NEW DEAL STUDIOS, INC.

Ian Hunter	David Sanger	Shannon Blake Gans
Forest P. Fischer	Scott Schneider	Branden W. Seifert
Scott Beverly	Robert Spurlock	John Cazin
Timothy E. Angulo	E.M. Bowen	Richard Slifka

Lidar Scanning by LIDAR VFX

Paul Maurice	Brandon Harr	Jon Hanzelka

Soundtrack Album on Reprise Records/WaterTower Music

"Non, Je Ne Regrette Rien"
Written by Charles Dumont and Michel Vaucaire
Performed by Edith Piaf
Courtesy of EMI Music France
Under license from EMI Film & Television Music

"Aboun Salehoun"
Written by Youssef El Mejjad and Pat Jabbar
Performed by Amira Saqati
Courtesy of Barraka el Farnatshi Productions

Filmed on location in Japan, United Kingdom, France, Morocco, USA and Canada

SPECIAL THANKS

City of Rancho Palos Verdes
La Prefecture de Police de Paris
La Mairie de Paris – Mission Cinema, Paris Film
His Majesty Mohamed VI and the Civilian and Military Authorities of Morocco
Audionamix Inc.
JR Train
© 2009 Estate of Francis Bacon. All Rights Reserved.

Filmed Partly on Location in Alberta, Canada with the Assistance of the
Government of Alberta, Alberta Film Development Program

Filmed on Location in France with the Assistance of the French Tax Rebate for
International Productions

Cameras & Lenses by PANAVISION ®

Camera Cranes and Dollies by CHAPMAN/LEONARD STUDIO EQUIPMENT, INC.

Color and Prints by TECHNICOLOR ®

No person or entity associated with this film received payment or anything of
value, or entered into any agreement, in connection with the depiction of tobacco
products.

Approved #46101

Motion Picture Association of America

This motion picture
© 2010 Warner Bros. Entertainment Inc. and Legendary Pictures
Story and Screenplay
© 2010 Warner Bros. Entertainment Inc.
Original Score
© 2010 Warner-Olive Music, LLC

INCEPTION

ABOUT THE
AUTHOR

CHRISTOPHER NOLAN began making movies at an early age with his father's Super-8mm camera. While studying English Literature at University College London, Nolan shot 16mm films at UCL's film society, learning the guerrilla film techniques he would later use to make his first feature, *Following*. Since that time, he has directed *Memento*, *Insomnia*, *Batman Begins*, *The Prestige*, and *The Dark Knight*. For his work on those films, Nolan has been honored with a Producer's Guild Nomination (*The Dark Knight*), a Writer's Guild Nomination (*The Dark Knight*), and two Director's Guild Nominations (*Memento*, *The Dark Knight*.) He also received Oscar® and Golden Globe® nominations for Best Screenplay for *Memento*. Nolan currently resides in Los Angeles with his wife and producer Emma Thomas, and their four children.